Compliments

COMPLIMENTS

A treasury of tributes ~
to friends and lovers, relatives and rivals

Compiled by Gertrude Buckman
Illustrated by Fiona Almeleh

The Bobbs-Merrill Company, Inc.
Indianapolis/New York

Compliments
was conceived and produced
by Imprint Books Limited
    12 Sutton Row, London, W1

Copyright © 1980 by Imprint Books Limited
All rights reserved including the
right of reproduction in whole or
in part in any form.

Published by The Bobbs-Merrill Company, Inc.
Indianapolis   New York

Library of Congress
Cataloging in Publication Data

Compliments.
    1. Quotations, English.   2. Compliments.
I. Buckman, Gertrude.
PN6084.C55C6   828'.02   80-678
ISBN 0-672-52650-6
D.L.: S.S. 281-80

Printed and bound in Spain
by TONSA San Sebastian

CONTENTS

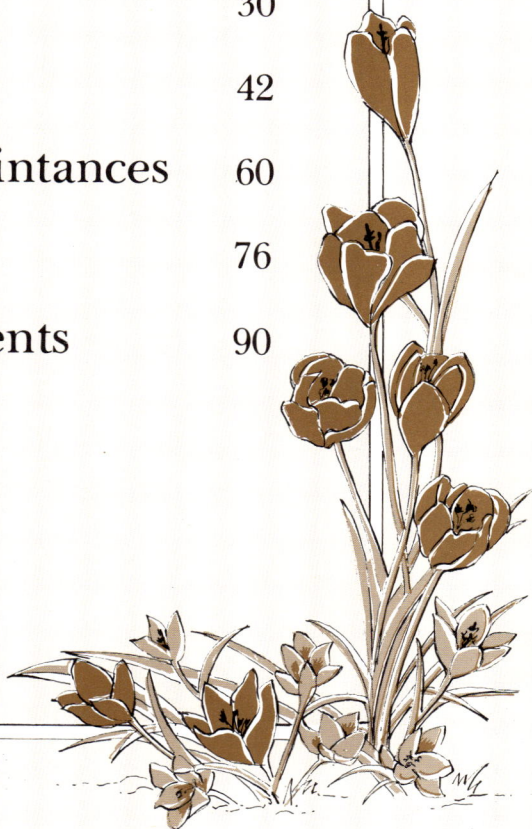

INTRODUCTION

Compliments soften hearts, bolster egos, cement old bonds, and establish new ones. They are the honey of life.

Surprisingly, compliments are not given as generously as might be imagined. The bewitched lover, for example, more often writes of his own needs and longings than of the outstanding qualities of his beloved. Women seem to be reserved about bestowing praise, perhaps because they feel that the deed speaks louder than the words. Parents compliment their children sparingly, possibly for fear of spoiling them. Children, only after they are well grown, may pay deserved tribute to their parents, but, alas, these are too often epitaphs. Friends and acquaintances offer praise for accomplishment, usually with great generosity. Sometimes, however, they succumb to temptation and their compliments are distinctly backhanded, although the wit of the remark can often alleviate the sting.

Thus a genuine, heartfelt compliment, penned by a poet in love or scribbled on the back of an envelope by a homesick youngster, whispered under a full moon, or written as a postscript to an otherwise prosaic letter, is precious—something to savour and to treasure.

[8]

Here are collected some of the most memorable compliments from different times and many places, paid by the famous, the infamous, the obscure, the unknown, to those they loved, respected, and admired. Some of these tributes express tenderness, others passion. Some are flowery, some are subtle, others are earthy and many are funny.

Some of these compliments are obviously calculated, their flattery motivated by ambition or greed. Undoubtedly, they were received with indifference or scorn except by the most insecure or vain. Most of the tributes in this collection, however, sprang from a sensitivity to special, individual virtues or charms. The balm of these true compliments could have given only pleasure.

Some writers pushed the sincerity of their passion to extravagant limits, out of obeisance to the literary conventions of their time or from sheer exuberance of emotion. Others gave praise with an economy of words and flourishes, but with eloquence born of deep feelings.

This is a book to be dipped into with pleasure, for each page yields a wealth of thought-provoking messages. It is also a source book, for it can be used when you are at a loss for the right words and know that someone, somewhere, sometime, must have aptly expressed just what you feel.

~ Men in Love ~

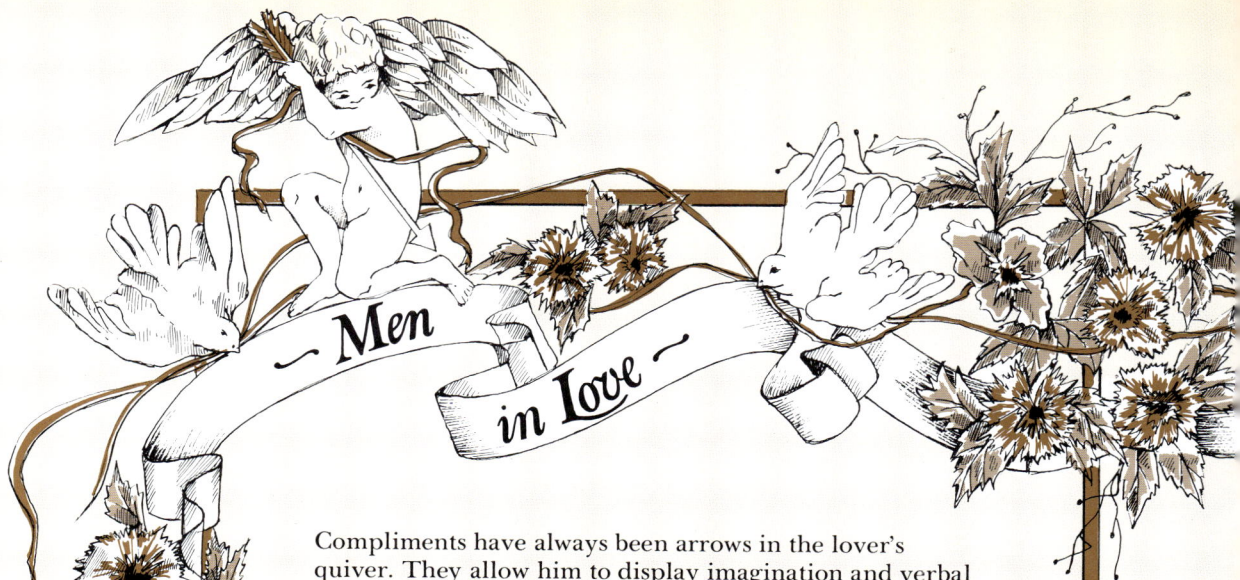

Compliments have always been arrows in the lover's quiver. They allow him to display imagination and verbal skills while at the same time softening his lady's heart with descriptions of her charms. Few writers, whatever their sexual inclinations, have not expressed their feelings in romantic or passionate tributes. The heightened language and extravagant metaphors of some of these could easily induce wonder and turn the coolest and most modest head. Yet some of the most ardent, like George Bernard Shaw's to the actress Ellen Terry, were never intended to be put to the test of actuality. These two were lovers only on paper; they dared not meet, and in fact a personal confrontation, in the end, finished off the "affair."

Others who experienced love—be it fulfilled, unrequited, or even imagined—have paid compliments that may be the most delightful of all, those which make up in sincerity what they may lack in grace or polish.

Although masculine praise has often been heavily canted towards physical attractions, such as the seventeenth-century poet's comparison of his beloved's face to a garden, later tributes tend to be more concerned with the whole woman. John Kennedy's short complimentary remark, for example, was singularly effective because it was a tribute to his wife's intelligence, charm, and poise.

[10]

Without thee I am all unblessed,
And wholly blessed in thee alone.
G. W. Bethune, American
editor, preacher, and
writer, in a poem dedicated
to his wife

You are a poem. Of what sort then? Epic? Mercy on me, no.
A sonnet? No, for that is too laboured and artificial. You are a
sort of sweet, simple, gay, pathetic ballad, which Nature is
singing, sometimes with tears, sometimes with smiles and
sometimes with intermingled smiles and tears.
Nathaniel Hawthorne, the American novelist,
to Sophie Amelia Peabody, whom he met in
1838, when he was thirty-four, and married
the following year

She is the violet,
The daisy delectable,
The columbine commendable,
The jelofer amiable;
For this most goodly flower,
This blossom of fresh colour,
So Jupiter me succour,
She flourisheth new, and new
In beauty and virtue.
John Skelton, fifteenth-century
English poet, in a poem
"The Commendation of Mistress Jane Scrope"

You are as beautiful, as witty, as prudent, and as good-humoured as any woman breathing. . . .

Sir Richard Steele, Irish essayist and dramatist, in a letter to his wife Mary Scurlock, his "dear Prue," in 1707, the year they married

She walks in beauty like the night
Of cloudless climes and starry skies;
And all that's best of dark and bright
Meet in her aspect and her eyes.

Lord Byron in a poem he wrote after seeing Mrs. Wilmot, a society beauty, in a dress of mourning with spangles on it

Health, my clear brain, and your fond love; and I feel that I can conquer the world.

Benjamin Disraeli to his fiancée Mary Anne Lewis, in a letter written shortly before their marriage

O thou art fairer than the evening air
Clad in the beauty of a thousand stars.

Christopher Marlowe, sixteenth-century English dramatist

She moves like a goddess, and she looks like a queen.

Homer, the ancient Greek poet, in the "Iliad"

Won't you come into the garden? I would like my roses to see you.
Richard Brinsley Sheridan, Irish
dramatist and parliamentary orator

You must believe me when I tell you that I have found it impossible to carry the heavy burden of responsibility and discharge my duties as king as I would wish to do without the help and support of the woman I love.
Edward VIII, in his radio broadcast to the people
of the United Kingdom when he abdicated to marry
Wallis Simpson, a commoner and a divorcée

You are wonderful.
Sir Arthur Conan Doyle to
his wife on his deathbed

You are always new. The last of your kisses was ever the sweetest; the last smile the brightest; the last movement the gracefullest.
John Keats, the English poet, in a letter to Fanny
Brawne whom he met shortly before he learned that
he had tuberculosis and would never be able to marry

I am the man who accompanied Jacqueline Kennedy to Paris, and I have enjoyed it.
President John F. Kennedy, in a comment made to the Paris
Press Club, in 1961, on the last day of an official visit,
when his wife was given an ecstatic reception by the French

[13]

She was a Phantom of delight
When first she gleamed upon my sight;
A lovely Apparition, sent
To be a moment's ornament; . . .
A perfect Woman, nobly planned,
To warm, to comfort, and command;
And yet a spirit still and bright,
With something of an angel-light.

William Wordsworth dedicated
this poem to his wife Mary

No Spring nor Summer Beauty hath such grace
As I have seen in one Autumnal face.

From John Donne's "Ninth Elegy" which
was dedicated to Lady Magdalen Herbert

. . . the thought of you sings, smiles, glows, and dances before
me like the sight of a cheerful fire, giving forth ever-changing
colours and penetrating heat, and in my memory I trace the
movements of your mouth when you speak.

Gustave Flaubert, the French
novelist, in a letter to his
mistress the poet Louise Colet

When I am with you, I leave aside my contemptuous,
suspicious nature.

James Joyce, the Irish writer, in a
letter to Nora Barnacle, the red-haired
girl from Galway who became his wife

Your name is like a golden bell
Hung in my heart; and when I think of you
I tremble, and the bell swings and rings. . . .
You know how, after looking at the sun
One sees red suns everywhere—so for hours
After the flood of sunshine that you are
My eyes are blinded by your burning hair. . . .

I had never known
Womanhood and its sweetness but for you.
> *Cyrano de Bergerac to Roxane, in Edmond*
> *Rostand's tragedy. Cyrano was a seventeenth-*
> *century soldier and poet who wooed the*
> *beautiful Roxane on behalf of a friend but*
> *secretly fell in love with her himself.*

I feel as if it would be flattering an angel to compare such a
being to you. You have been privileged to receive every gift
from nature, you have both fortitude and tears.
> *Victor Hugo, the French writer, to Adele Foucher,*
> *in a letter of 1822, the year they were married.*
> *He was twenty, she was nineteen, and they had*
> *been secretly engaged for three years.*

Shall I compare thee to a summer's day?
Thou art more lovely and more temperate.
William Shakespeare, Sonnet 18

. . . if we never met again in our lives I should feel that somehow
the whole adventure of existence was justified by my having met you.
> *Lewis Mumford, American author, in a*
> *letter to his wife before their marriage*

You could give yourself to another, but none could love you more purely or more completely than I did. To none could your happiness be holier, as it was to me, and always will be. My whole experience, everything that lives within me, everything, my most precious, I devote to you, and if I try to ennoble myself, this is done in order to become ever worthier of you, to make you ever happier.

Johann Christoph Friedrich von Schiller,
eighteenth-century German poet and dramatist, to
Lotte von Lengefeld in 1789, the year before they married

There's nothing that I will not brave for your sake;
you deserve much more than that.

Voltaire, the French eighteenth-century
writer, to Olympe Dunoyer

One smile from her lips will never be forgot,
It refreshes, like a shower from a watering pot.

She's my myrtle, my geranium,
My sun flower, my sweet marjoram,
My honey suckle, my tulip, my violet,
My holly hock, my dahlia, my mignonette.

She's my snowdrop, my ranunculus,
My hyacinth, my gilliflower, my polyanthus,
My heart's ease, my pink water lily,
My buttercup, my daisy lily, my daffydown dilly.

From "The Broken Hearted Gardener,"
a nineteenth-century ballad

When you were here there was no other person whom I liked better to see; and now when you are gone there is no other person whom I would so fain see again.... I have had some remarkably fine tours this year, both in the Highlands and in England, and fell acquainted with some very fine ladies, but as soon as I got from them, the black-eyed Nithsdale lassie was always uppermost in my mind.... I might perhaps get a better wife or a richer wife, but I find I could not get one I like so well, or that would suit me better.

James Hogg, Scottish poet, to Margaret Phillips,
the girl he married in 1820 when he was fifty years old

Was this the face that launched a thousand ships,
And burnt the topless towers of Ilium?
Sweet Helen, make me immortal with a kiss!

Christopher Marlowe

Her personal appearance has nothing to do with the hold she has upon my mind, for I have seen hundreds of prettier women. But I never met with so sweet a temper, so self-sacrificing and affectionate a disposition, or so pure and womanly a mind....

Thomas Henry Huxley, biologist and educator,
father of Julian and Aldous, to his mother
about his fiancée, Henrietta Anne Heathorn,
whom he had met in Australia and soon married

The sweetest flower that blows
    I give you as we part;
For you it is a rose
    For me it is my heart.

Frederick Peterson, American poet,
physician, and university professor

She is a very superior woman, and very little spoiled, which is strange in an heiress—a girl of twenty—a peeress that is to be, in her own right—an old child, and a savante, who has always had her own way.... She is a poetess—a mathematician—a metaphysician, and yet, withal, very kind, generous, and gentle, with very little pretension.... Any other head would be turned with half her acquisitions, and a tenth of her advantages.

Lord Byron about Annabella Milbanke,
to whom he was briefly married

My dear, my better half.
Sir Philip Sidney, sixteenth-century
English poet, statesman, and soldier

When I married Nancy, I hitched my wagon to a star and when I got into the House of Commons in 1910 I found that I had hitched my wagon to a shooting star.

In 1944, the second Viscount Astor said this
in a speech about his American wife, who became
the first woman to sit in the British Parliament

I have seen only you, I have admired only you, I desire only you.
Napoleon Bonaparte
to Marie Walewska

There is a garden in her face,
    Where roses and white lilies blow;
A heavenly paradise is that place,
    Wherein all pleasant fruits do grow.
From a seventeenth-century poem

[18]

She's all my fancy painted her;
She's love, she's divine.

From the poem, "Alice Gray,"
by the nineteenth-century
English poet William Mee

Your uncommon personal advantages and your superior good taste
do not so much strike me. These possibly may be met with in a
few instances in others; but that amiable goodness, that tender
feminine softness, that endearing sweetness of disposition with
all the charming offspring of a warm, feeling heart—these I never
again expect to meet with, in such a degree, in this world.

Robert Burns, to Ellison Begbie, the servant
girl who was his first love. His love letters
to her are the earliest examples of his prose.

The finest woman in nature should not detain me an hour from
you; but you must sometimes suffer the rivalship of the wisest men.

Sir Richard Steele to Mary Scurlock
in 1712, after five years of marriage

In white dresses and large hats, with parasols in their hands,
their beauty literally took one's breath away, for suddenly
seeing them one stopped astonished and everything including one's
breathing for one second also stopped as it does when in a picture
gallery you suddenly come face to face with a great Rembrandt or
Velasquez. . . . It was almost impossible for a man not to fall in
love with them, and I think I did that at once.

Leonard Woolf, English publisher and writer, about
his first sight of the sisters Virginia and
Vanessa Stephen; Virginia later became his wife.

We have not been separated for three and thirty years and, during all that time, in her society I never have had a moment of dullness.

Benjamin Disraeli, prime minister of Great
Britain and author, about his wife Mary Anne

Never so happily in one
    Did heaven and earth combine.
And yet 'tis flesh and blood alone
    That makes her so divine.

Thomas D'Urfey, English song-writer
and dramatist, to "Chloe Divine"

If you do not believe my tongue, consult my eyes, consult your own. You will find by yours that they have charms, by mine that I have a heart which feels them. . . . Love, almighty love, seems in a moment to have removed me to a prodigious distance from every object but you alone. In the midst of crowds I remain in solitude. Nothing but you can lay hold of my mind, and that can lay hold of nothing but you. I appear transported to some foreign desert with you (oh that I were really thus transported), where, abundantly supplied with everything, in this, I might live out an age of uninterrupted ecstasy. . . . Unlovely objects are all around me, excepting thee; the charms of all the world appear to be translated to thee.

William Congreve, English dramatist,
to Arabella Hunt, a singer

I love you soulfully and bodyfully, properly and improperly, every way that a woman can be loved.

George Bernard Shaw, Irish playwright, to Ellen Terry,
the English actress with whom he had an epistolary romance

In thy face I have seen the eternal.
Baron Christian von Bunsen, nineteenth-century Prussian diplomat and scholar, to his wife on his deathbed

My own dearest beloved wife—your reminder of our wedding day brought the tears into my eyes; for though I may be inattentive to such anniversaries generally, my heart must be made of stone not to care, to mind and contrast the happiness experienced on that blessed day. . . . Believe me, my darling Lizzie, when I swear that my love for you is as true at this moment as it was eighteen years ago.
Charles James Mathews, nineteenth-century English actor, playwright, and architect, to his wife Lucia Elizabeth, an actress and singer known as Madame Vestris, on July 8, 1838, from prison in Lancaster

Do not conceale no beauty, grace,
That's either in thy minde or face.. . .
Sir Francis Kynaston, seventeenth-century English poet, in a poem, "To Cynthia. On Concealment of her Beauty"

Age cannot wither her, nor custom stale
Her infinite variety; other women cloy
The appetites they feed; but she makes hungry
Where most she satisfies. . . .
Enobarbus about Cleopatra in Shakespeare's "Antony and Cleopatra"

Believe me, if all those endearing young charms,
    Which I gaze on so fondly today
Were to change by tomorrow, and fleet in my arms,
    Like fairy gifts fading away!
Thou wouldst still be ador'd as this moment thou art,
    Let thy loveliness fade as it will.
                    Thomas Moore,
                    nineteenth-century Irish poet

She is pretty to walk with,
And witty to talk with,
And pleasant too, to think on.
        Sir John Suckling,
        seventeenth-century Cavalier poet

The dimple that thy chin contains has beauty in its round,
That never has been fathomed yet by myriad thoughts profound.
                Hafiz, fourteenth-century
                Persian poet and mystic philosopher

Please suggest a remedy to stop me trembling with joy like a lunatic
when I receive and read your letters. . . . You have given me a gift
such as I never even dreamt of finding in this life.
                Franz Kafka, Czech writer, to Felice Bauer,
                who became his fiancée, but never his wife

She is as nice, as lovable, and amiable and charming in every
way as she is beautiful, and by her education and bringing up
she is in every way qualified to fill any position.
            Randolph Churchill, the British statesman, in a
            letter to his father about his fiancée, the American
            beauty Jennie Jerome, whom he married in 1874

Love in her sunny eyes does basking play;
Love walks the pleasant mazes of her hair;
Love does on both her lips forever stray;
And sows and reaps a thousand kisses there.
Abraham Cowley, English metaphysical poet

My fairest, my espoused, my latest found,
Heaven's last best gift, my ever new delight. . . .
*John Milton, English poet, in "Paradise Lost," about
his third wife Elizabeth whom he married in 1663
when she was twenty-five and he was fifty-five*

From the day that I first spoke to her I never had
a thought of her ever being the wife of any other man.
*William Cobbett, eighteenth-century
English journalist and social reformer*

Thou all sweetness dost enclose,
Like a little world of bliss.
*Thomas Campion, English lyricist
and lutanist, in a song to a lady*

I feel myself eternally bound to the woman three times blessed who
cherished me and saved me from myself. I love thee with my head,
my heart, and my senses. I love thee to infinity.
*Léon Gambetta, one of the most powerful men
in France in the middle of the nineteenth century,
to Léonie Léon with whom he had a secret
lifelong liaison*

[23]

See! how she leans her cheek upon her hand:
O! that I were a glove upon that hand,
That I might touch that cheek.

Romeo about Juliet

I have arrived here safe and sound except for the hole in my heart,
which you have made, like a dear, enchanting slut as you are . . . and
now, my dear, dear girl! let me assure you of the truest friendship
for you that ever man bore towards a woman. Wherever I am, my
heart is warm towards you and ever shall be till it is cold forever.

Laurence Sterne, eighteenth-century
British novelist, to Catherine Formantel

She is the only woman in France who makes me forget
I am a sexagenarian.

Louis XV of France
about his mistress Mme. du Barry

Though you reprove me with some vehemence, it is at the same time
in so friendly, and so reasonable, a manner that I kiss the rod
which beats me and give you as sincere thanks for your admonitions
as ever I did for any of your civilities and services.

David Hume, eighteenth-century Scottish
philosopher and historian, to Mme. de Boufflers

Ah, love,—you are my unutterable blessing. . . . I am
in full sunshine now.

Robert Browning, English poet, to his wife
Elizabeth Barrett Browning, the poet

You are a very charming woman, and I should be happy to obtain you as a wife.

Samuel Parr, eighteenth-century English
schoolmaster, to Miss Jane Morsingale

When naked both, thou seemest not to be
Contiguous, but continuous parts of me.

Sir Francis Kynaston, in
"To Cynthia, on Her Embraces"

My own dear boy—Your sonnet is quite lovely and it is a marvel that those red roseleaf lips of yours should be made no less for the music of song than for the madness of kissing.

Oscar Wilde, the Irish poet, wit,
and dramatist, to Lord Alfred Douglas

Go, lovely rose,
    Tell her that wastes her time and me,
    That now she knows,
    When I resemble her to thee,
    How sweet and fair she seems to be.

Edmund Waller, seventeenth-
century English poet

Oh, my Lolita! . . . a ray of sunshine at the break of day! As a stream of light in an obscure night.

Ludwig I of Bavaria to Lola Montez, the dancer
and adventuress

Thou art my life, my love, my heart,
The very eyes of me:
And hast command of every part,
To live and die for thee.
Robert Herrick, the seventeenth-century
English lyric poet, "To Anthea"

I think of the rare perfection of her who was at birth so aptly
named Eve, for she is unique on earth; there cannot be another so
angelic, no other woman who could embody more gentleness, more
ingenuity, more love, more inspiration in her caresses.
Honoré de Balzac, the nineteenth-century French
novelist, in a letter of 1840 to the Polish
Countess Hanska, five years before they married

Beautiful in form and feature
Lovely as the day,
Can there be so fair a creature
Formed of common clay?
Henry Wadsworth Longfellow,
nineteenth-century American poet

If I could write the beauty of your eyes
And in fresh numbers number all your graces,
The age to come would say, "This poet lies;
Such heavenly touches ne'er touch'd earthly faces."
William Shakespeare, Sonnet 17

Believe me, sweet heart, thy kindness is as necessary to comfort
my heart as thy assistance is for my affairs.
King Charles II to the Queen Consort, Henrietta Maria

I go about murmuring, "I have made that dignified girl *commit* herself, I have, I have," and then I vault over the sofa with exultation.

Walter Bagehot, nineteenth-century
English economist, essayist, and
journalist, to Elizabeth Wilson in
1857, the year before they married

Nelson's Alpha and Omega is Emma! . . . I feel that you are the real friend of my bosom, and dearer to me than life.

Horatio, Lord Nelson, British naval hero,
to his mistress, Emma, Lady Hamilton

Sensual pleasure passes and vanishes in the twinkling of an eye, but the friendship between us, the mutual confidence, the delights of the heart, the enchantment of the soul, these things do not perish and can never be destroyed. I shall love you until I die.

Voltaire to Mme. Denis, one of his mistresses

Her lips they are redder than coral
That under the ocean grows;
She is sweet, she is fair, she is moral,
My beautiful Georgian rose!

Anonymous

I anticipate with you the pleasure we shall enjoy when we have no third person to break in upon our sweet house of social and conjugal happiness. I have a thousand things to say to you. I think, write, talk, work, love—all, all—only for you.

Benjamin Rush, eighteenth-century
American physician, politician, and
humanitarian, to his wife, Julia

By Saint Mary, my lady,
Your mammy and your daddy
Brought forth a goodly baby!
*John Skelton in a poem
to Mistress Isabel Pennell*

The hours I spend with you I look upon as a sort of perfumed garden, a dim twilight, and a fountain singing to it . . . you and you *alone* make me feel that I am alive. . . . Other men it is said have seen angels, but I have seen thee and thou art enough.
*George Moore, Irish novelist,
to Lady Emerald Cunard*

All time is worse than lost that's spent where thou art not, thou only relish to all other pleasures. Tis you alone that sweetens life. . . .
*John Hervey, First Earl of Bristol,
to his first wife Elizabeth*

I am not now indifferent to wealth or power or place in the world's eye. I would fain be rich, that I might render you comfortable; powerful, that I might raise you to those high places of society which you are so fitted to adorn; celebrated, that the world might justify your choice.
*Hugh Miller, nineteenth-century Scottish geologist
and man of letters, to his wife Lydia*

She has made me half in love with a cold climate.
*Robert Southey, the English poet, in a letter
of 1797, about Edith, his wife of two years*

When, dearest, I but think of thee,
Methinks all things that lovely be
Are present, and my soul delighted.
Sir John Suckling

To me you are the gate of paradise. For you I will renounce
fame, creativity, everything.
*Frederick Chopin, the Polish composer and
pianist, to his mistress Delphine Potocka*

There was such goodness, such pure nature seen
In Lucy's looks, a manner so serene;
Such harmony in motion, speech, and air,
That without fairness she was more than fair,
Had more than beauty in each speaking grace,
That lent their cloudless glory to the face. . . .
*George Crabbe, English poet;
"Lucy" is thought to have
been inspired by Sarah Elmy,
whom he married.*

Your character is marked with virtues all original (and such
as would naturally excite curiosity and respect).
*Warren Hastings, English statesman and administrator
in India, to his wife. They had met on a ship going to
India in 1769 and married eight years later.*

You'd break a Lent with looking on her.
John Cleveland, seventeenth-century English poet

[29]

Women in Love

Among the poetic sounds of the past there are relatively few women's voices. This is not because women have ever lacked passion or disdained love.

For centuries, the chivalric tradition encouraged women to sit back on their pedestals and enjoy, rather than bestow, compliments. Those who flouted convention were most likely to do so quietly, almost in secrecy. Perhaps loving deeds more than loving words have been women's principal way of paying tribute and giving praise.

Women of past generations, who complimented their lovers lavishly and openly, tended to be unconventional in their approach to life. Isabel Burton, for example, was a proper Victorian girl who married a remarkable and eccentric explorer and for thirty years of happy marriage accompanied him and worked at his side in the most unlikely parts of the world and in the most uncomfortable circumstances. After his death she built a tomb that was a stone replica of the tent they shared in their wanderings. Of the same calibre was the spirited Hester Thrale, Dr. Samuel Johnson's great friend, who, when she was eighty years old, fell in love with a young actor and unabashedly paid tribute to him.

Compliments given by women to their lovers are among the rarest, and are therefore the most precious. Those that have been made public are gems—valuable and memorable.

I would rather have a crust and a tent with you than be queen of all the world.

Isabel Burton to her husband Richard, the colourful nineteenth-century explorer and writer. She shared his wanderings from the time of their marriage in 1861 until his death thirty years later, writing travel books, and his biography.

I am sorry you had bad sport, and I shall be most happy to see you at home, to warm you with my kisses, and comfort you with my smiles and good humer, and oblidge you by my attentions, which will be the constant pleasure of my Dear Sir William.

Emma to Sir William Hamilton in 1787, four years before they married

My love is fairer than a summer day,
His breath it is sweeter than newly mown hay.

An old Irish song

I like his ways. He is light on his feet and moves about with assurance. . . . He applies his entire mind to what he is doing, he puts his entire soul into getting me a glass of water or lighting my cigarette. He never makes me lose my temper. He is punctual, he has a watch and he takes the trouble to glance at it.

French novelist George Sand about her last lover Alexandre Manceau, with whom she lived happily for fifteen years until his death in 1865

[31]

Your youth and strength are full in perfection.... Good night! and God bless my dearest and most valued friend.

Hester Thrale Piozzi, Dr. Samuel Johnson's
friend, to William August Conway,
a young actor with whom she fell in love
when she was eighty years old

I cannot love you and be perfectly satisfied at such a distance from you.

Elizabeth Ann Sheridan to her
husband Richard Brinsley Sheridan

How on earth have you mastered the art of being subtle, profound, humorous, arch, coy, satirical, affectionate, intimate, profane, colloquial, solemn, sensible, poetical, and a dear old shabby sheepdog—on the wireless?

Virginia Woolf to Vita Sackville-West, writer and
notable gardener, after hearing her broadcast

In some few months, it will be four years that I am so happy and still I dote on him as if he were my bridegroom. He is good, really good, in all his actions, in all the foldings of his heart.

Margaret Klopstock about her husband
Frederick Gottlieb Klopstock, the German epic poet

It is you who have just given sensibility and life to my heart. Since I loved you my friends are dearer to me; I love myself more.

Ninon de Lenclos, French courtesan of the
seventeenth century, to the Marquis de Sévigné

All that he has to say seems so good and glorious. . . .

Mary James of her husband Henry James,
the father of Henry, the novelist,
and William, the philosopher

Cherish me with that dignified tenderness which I have only
found in you. . . .

Mary Wollstonecraft, English feminist writer,
to Gilbert Imlay, the American who was
her lover and the father of her first child

How often do I reflect with pleasure that I hold in possession
a Heart Equally warm with my own, and fully as Susceptable of the
Tenderest impressions, and who even now, whilst he is reading
here, feels all I describe.

Abigail Smith Adams in a letter to
her husband John Adams, the second
president of the United States

You were born under a happy star, you are gay, you have many
talents, you are at ease everywhere, you are completely
self-sufficient.

Marquise de Deffand (Marie de Vichy
Chamraud) a famous salonnière,
during the reign of Louis XV, in
a letter of 1771 to Horace Walpole,
who was twenty years her junior

To my dear husband . . . I give this manuscript of a work which would never have been written but for the happiness which his love has conferred on my life.

George Eliot, the English novelist, in 1859, in her dedication of "Adam Bede" to George Henry Lewes with whom she lived until his death but never married

He is among the cleverest men of his day; not the cleverest only but the most enlightened! He possesses all the qualities I deem essential in my Husband, a warm true heart to love me, a towering intellect to command me, and a spirit of fire to be the guiding star of my life . . . a wise and noble man, one who holds his patent of nobility from Almighty God, whose high stature of manhood is not to be measured by the inch rule of Lilliputs!

Jane Baillie Welsh about Thomas Carlyle, the Scottish writer whom she was to marry

I need your love as a touchstone of my existence. It is the sun which breathes life into me.

Juliette Drouet to her lover Victor Hugo, the French author

Don't ever think of the things you can't give me—You've trusted me with the dearest heart of all—and it's so damn much more than anybody else in all the world has ever had.

Zelda Sayre to American writer F. Scott Fitzgerald shortly before their marriage

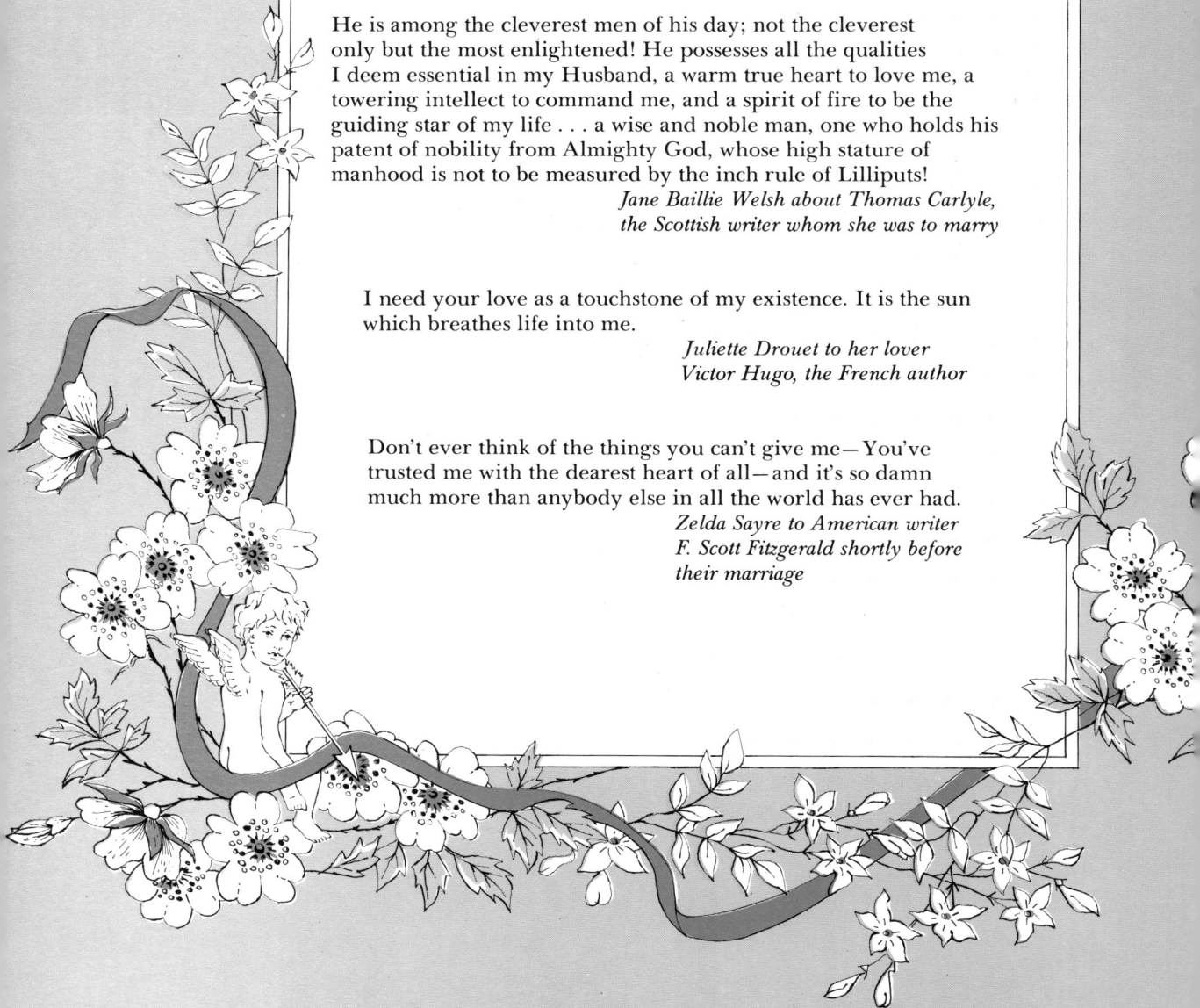

His words are bonds, his oaths are oracles;
His love sincere, his thoughts immaculate;
His tears, pure messengers sent from his heart;
His heart as far from fraud as heaven from earth.
Julia describing her lover Proteus,
in Shakespeare's "Two Gentlemen of Verona"

I know that you have not bathed without everyone on that
hot island desiring you . . . that they could follow the glimmer
of your perfect form to the ends of the earth
Natalie Barney, American writer and
art patron in Paris between the wars,
to her lover, the painter Romaine Brooks

. . . being mortal, this luxurious heart
Would starve for you, my dear, I must admit,
If it were held another hour apart
From that food which alone can comfort it—
I am come home to you, for at the end
I find I cannot live without you, friend.
May Sarton, American poet and novelist

I know your good nature is such that you cannot see any
human creature miserable without being sensibly touched. . . .
Nor is the love I bear you only seated in my soul, for there
is not a single atom of my frame that is not blended with it.
Therefore don't flatter yourself that separation will ever
change my sentiments.

Vanessa (Esther Vanhomrigh) to
Jonathan Swift, Irish-born satirist

Your fun comes spouting out "all alive oh." All sparkle.
Young, strong. It catches hold of one, shakes one, wakes
one! And however devilish you may choose to try to appear,
in the end you are all heavenly!

Ellen Terry to George Bernard Shaw

M. d'Arblay is one of the most singularly interesting characters
that can ever have been formed . . . a man open as the day—warmly
affectionate to his friends—intelligent, ready, amusing in
conversation, with a great share of *gaieté de coeur* . . . a sincerity,
a frankness, an ingenuous openness of nature. . . .

Fanny Burney, nineteenth-century novelist
most celebrated for "Evelina," about
Lafayette's adjutant-general, with whom
she fell in love at the age of forty-one,
married, and lived with happily

Strephon's kiss was lost in jest,
Robin's lost in play,
But the kiss in Colin's eyes
Haunts me night and day.

Sara Teasdale, American poet

I feel more powerfully all those so-termed sexual impulses with
her than I have with any man. . . . I feel that to lie with my head
on her breast is to feel what life can hold. All my troubles,
my wretched fears, are swept away . . . gone the terrible banality
of my life. Nothing remains except the shelter of her arms.

Katherine Mansfield, English writer.
about a woman who was her lover

To his whole era, he was good news, a day off, A.W.O.L. But most of all—with his many gifts and his child's heart—Charlie was really Christmas.

Helen Hayes, the American actress, about
Charles MacArthur, her writer husband

I fear more for your dear person than for my poor carcass. I know who is most necessary in the world. What I fear most at present is not hearing from you. Love me whatever happens and be assured I am ever entirely yours till death!

Queen Mary II of England (daughter of
James II) to her husband William of Orange
who was fighting in Ireland in 1690

But what could resist you? Your reputation, which so much attracts the vanity of our sex, your air, your manner, that light in your eyes which expresses the vivacity of your mind, your conversation so easy and elegant that it gave everything you said an agreeable turn, in short, everything spoke for you.

From a convent in 1128, Heloise wrote to Abelard,
the most famous philosopher of his age and her
former tutor and husband. Upon discovering their
marriage, her uncle, in vicious revenge, had Abelard
castrated. The couple entered religious orders, but
continued to correspond until their deaths.

Certainly if you are not as happy as anyone could be, at least you are more loved than anyone has ever been.

Mme. Staal de Launay, a Frenchwoman
noted for her wit and her many lovers,
to the Chevalier de Menil

I might call him
A thing divine—for nothing natural
I ever saw so noble.
Miranda at her first sight of Ferdinand,
in Shakespeare's "The Tempest"

Your words dispel all the care in the world and make me
happy. . . . They are as necessary to me now as sunlight and air . . . .
Your words are my food, your breath my wine—you are everything
to me.

Sarah Bernhardt, French actress,
to Victorien Sardou, French poet
and playwright

I find in you a kindness, an honesty that will give you—for ever—
a right over my soul which you have filled with gratitude, *esteem,*
with sensibility, and with all the sentiments that put intimacy and
confidence in a friendship . . . your character destines you to be
great—your talents condemn you to celebrity . . . some names were made
to be written in history; yours will, one day, excite admiration.
Julie de Lespinasse, eighteenth-
century French intellectual, to
the Comte de Guibert who was
eleven years younger than she
and became her lover

Say to yourself that your talent is incomparable, determine
its course, but do not doubt its power.
Mme. de Staël in 1814 to her
lover and protegé Benjamin Constant,
a writer and politician

To have lived with and worked for him makes ordinary life seem humdrum and ridiculous.

> *Faith Mackenzie, English writer and sculptor,*
> *about her husband, the writer Compton Mackenzie*

My sensations are so new to me that while I acknowledge their power, I cannot define them . . . tell yourself that you are of all the men in the world the most tenderly loved. . . . Though I am not vain it was impossible not to feel flattered by all this talk about you—I could not take a step without hearing your eulogies! —and these were given in a fashion that did, I must admit, seduce my ear and touch my heart.

> *Judith Charlotte de Biron, Comtesse de Bonneval,*
> *to her husband, a brilliant and popular foreign*
> *service man in the first half of the eighteenth*
> *century. He married her when he was forty-two,*
> *she seventeen, and, after ten days of marriage,*
> *left her and never saw her again*

He appreciates better than any man I know the value of a woman who has something to give in return for being given to.

> *Mary Anne Disraeli about her*
> *husband Benjamin Disraeli*

My beloved is white and ruddy, the chiefest
    among ten thousand. . . .
His mouth is most sweet: yea, he is altogether
    lovely.
This is my beloved, and this is my friend.

> *Song of Solomon*

He is a perfect angel—only more to the point than most angels—
I should have shot myself long ago . . . if it hadn't been for him.
*Virginia Woolf, the English writer, about
her husband Leonard*

When you are there it will be paradise.
*Emma, Lady Hamilton to her lover
Horatio, Lord Nelson*

I shall ever remember the gentleness of your manners and the
wild originality of your countenance. Having been once seen,
you are not to be forgotten.
*Jane Clairmont to Lord Byron.
Jane, who accompanied Mary Godwin when
she ran off with Percy Bysshe Shelley, bore
Byron's daughter, Allegra.*

Whether I marry you or not I shall always think of you as the
only man I could have married & the only man I ever really loved.
*Jennie Jerome to her
fiancé Lord Randolph Churchill*

I need all eternity to love you in.
*Jill Furse, English actress, to her husband
Laurence Whistler, the English poet, in 1944,
the year before she died at the age of thirty*

I bless God for the choice I have made. My admiration of his character increases daily. This feeling of perfect confidence in the nobility of soul of the man one marries is a great happiness.

Albertine de Staël, daughter of the French writer Mme. de Staël, just after her marriage in 1816 to the French nobleman Victor de Broglie

You are all that is good and kind.... You were made perfectly to be loved.

Elizabeth Barrett Browning to her husband Robert Browning

I do not love thee!—no! I do not love thee! And yet when thou art absent I am sad.

Caroline Norton, nineteenth-century English author and the granddaughter of Richard Brinsley Sheridan

He was the most interesting man I've ever met.

Lillian Hellman, the American playwright, about Dashiell Hammett, the writer, whom she loved for more than thirty years

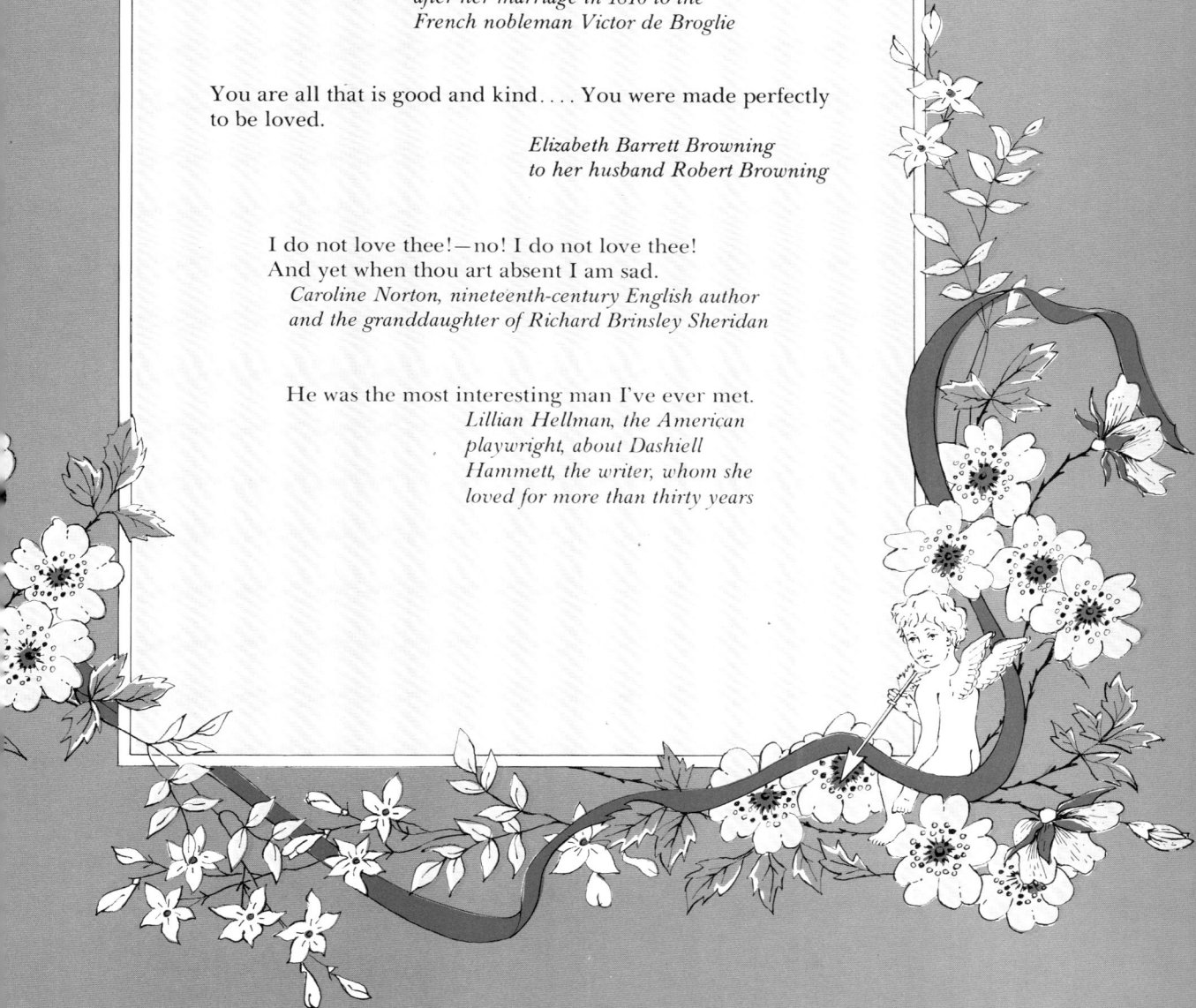

Kissing Kin

How familiar the term "nuclear family" is today—and how bleak and comfortless a ring it has. But say "extended family," and at once images are evoked of bulging snapshot albums, of happy reunions, of a web of correspondence, images of support, reassurance, and warmth. For those who are fortunate, kinship connection means that someone will certainly be on hand in times of crisis as well as of celebration.

But relatives also tend to take one another for granted and to be miserly with the coin of compliment. It is lovely and refreshing, therefore, to find touching family tributes. It is delightful to discover that sons and daughters do praise parents, as Louisa May Alcott did when she sent her mother a copy of her first book. It is pleasant to find siblings ungrudgingly complimenting each other—as writer Henry James did his philosopher brother William, or the poet Christina Rossetti her sister.

And since parents have seemed, at times, a little reluctant to admit in so many words how dear to them their offspring really are, how heartwarming is the uninhibited praise given to Evangeline Booth of the Salvation Army by her father, or Alexandre Dumas's tribute to his natural son.

Here you will find, too, praises of cousins, aunts, uncles, grandchildren, grandparents, nieces, and nephews, as well as of in-laws and step-parents—all members of extended families.

My name-son, a bright and blue-eyed rogue, with flaxen hair, screams and laughs like an April morning; and the baby is that species of dough which is called a fine baby.

Sir Walter Scott, Scottish writer, about his grandchildren

Living with her was like being on a journey of discovery that never ended.

Elizabeth Goudge, British novelist, about her mother

Amongst the other innumerable blessings, I must not forget the bounty of Heaven in granting you a mind that rejoices in the practice of those eminent virtues which form great and good characters. . . . The height of glory to which your professional judgement, united with a proper degree of bravery, guarded by Providence, has raised you, few sons, my dear child, attain to, and few fathers live to see.

Edmund Nelson, a parish vicar, in a letter to his son Horatio, who had just become a national hero after the Battle of St. Vincent

I was so proud of you and thrilled at having you so close to me on our long walk in Westminster Abbey, but when I handed your hand to the Archbishop I felt I had lost something very precious.

George VI of England in a letter to his daughter, Princess Elizabeth, just after her marriage to Philip Mountbatten

[43]

There is simplicity in his character that charms me.
William Cowper, eighteenth-century
English poet, about one of his kinsmen

Your heart, I have no doubt, has blessed and cheered and delighted
the soul of the mother who bore you, from the very first opening
of your eyes upon the world, and that dear heart has gone on with
that cheering influence from that time to the present and it will
go on cheering everybody around you who has loved you.
General William Booth, founder of the Salvation Army,
in a letter to his daughter Evangeline in 1912, when
she was in command of the Salvation Army in America

Fifty-four years of love and tenderness and crossness and devotion
and unswerving loyalty. Without her I could only have achieved a
quarter of what I have achieved, not only in terms of success and
career, but in terms of personal happiness. . . . She has never stood
between me and my life, never tried to hold me too tightly, always
let me go free. . . .
Noel Coward, British dramatist, about his mother

You are truly my son, and not only my son, but well-nigh the
only happiness and distraction that I have.
Alexandre Dumas, the nineteenth-century
French novelist and playwright, in a letter
to his natural and only son Alexandre

I copied him, I loved him, I wanted to be him.
Leo Tolstoi, Russian author.
about his brother Sergei

[44]

My dearest child, we do miss you sadly, and though no doubt you did give us occasionally trouble—you ever possessed those great qualities of heart and head which have made you the object of such interest and love and affection and the last three weeks you were all the fondest mother could wish.

> *Queen Victoria to her eldest daughter shortly after her marriage to Prince Frederick of Prussia in 1858*

For there is no friend like a sister
In calm or stormy weather;
To cheer one on the tedious way,
To fetch one if one goes astray,
To lift one if one totters down,
To strengthen whilst one stands.

> *Christina Rossetti, English poet, to her sister Maria Francesca, who entered an Anglican sisterhood*

It is very exciting—the extreme potency of your brats; they might have been nincompoops instead of bubbling and boiling and frizzling like so many pans of sausages on the fire.

> *Virginia Woolf about her nephews, Julian and Quentin Bell, in a letter to her sister Vanessa*

I assure you that I have never received one of your dear letters without regretting, with tears in my eyes, that I am separated from such a tender and good mother, and though I am happy enough here, I still ardently wish that I could return to see my dear, my very dear family. . . .

> *Marie Antoinette, doomed French queen, to her mother, Maria Theresa, Empress of Austria*

Then farewell, my dear, my loved daughter, adieu;
The last pang of life is in parting from you.
Thomas Jefferson, third president
of the United States, in a deathbed
poem to his daughter

Thirty-four years of unbroken kindness, of cloudless sunshine, of perpetual joy, of constant love. Thirty-four years of happy smiles, of loving looks and gentle words, of generous deeds. Thirty-four years, a flower, a palm, a star, a faultless child, a perfect woman, wife, and mother.
Robert G. Ingersoll, the nineteenth-
century American lecturer, in a note
to his daughter Eva on her birthday

Whatever beauty or poetry is to be found in my little book is owing to your interest in and encouragement of all my efforts from the first to the last, and if ever I do anything to be proud of, my greatest happiness will be that I can thank you for that, as I may do for all the good that is in me.
Louisa May Alcott, American writer,
in a Christmas letter to her
mother in 1854 accompanying a copy
of her first book "Flower Fable"

I am not only your brother, your friend, but at the same time I have infinite obligations of gratitude to you. Money can be repaid, but not kindness such as yours.
Vincent van Gogh, Dutch painter,
in a letter to his brother Theo

Yes, my beloved, be my genius, my solace, my companion, my joy . . .
we will feel that life can never be a blank while gilded by the
perfect love of a sister and a brother.

Benjamin Disraeli to his sister Sarah

You appear to me so superior, so elevated above other men,
I contemplate you with such a strange mixture of humility,
admiration, reverence, love, and pride, that very little
superstition would be necessary to make me worship you as
a superior being. . . . I had rather not live than not be the
daughter of such a man.

*Theodosia Burr, in a letter to her father Aaron
Burr, the American revolutionary officer and
political leader who became vice-president of
the United States*

I want very, very much a little of your wit my dear sister—a
letter or two of yours just to bandy back a pun or two across
the Atlantic and send a quibble over the Floridas.

*John Keats, English poet, to
his sister-in-law Georgiana*

I am deeply touched by your tenderness for me, when it would
be so natural for you to be absorbed by another feeling. Your
image mingles with all my reveries; it is through you that I
have a future.

*Mme. Récamier, French society leader, to her
niece Mme. Lenormant, who was waiting for
a ship to take her to her husband in Greece*

Intreat me not to leave thee, or to return from following after thee: for wither thou goest, I will go; and where thou lodgest, I will lodge: thy people shall be my people, and thy God my God: Where thou diest, will I die, and there will I be buried: the Lord do so to me and more also, if ought but death part thee and me.

Ruth to her mother-in-law Naomi in the Old Testament

My ambition is to be corrected and converted by you my whole life long without ever becoming completely corrected or converted.

Leo Tolstoi to his Aunt Alexandra

All that I am or hope to be, I owe to my angel mother.

Abraham Lincoln

If others were observant, she missed nothing.

William Plomer, South African novelist and poet, about his grandmother

That's the kind of mother to have, the kind I had, credulous, superstitious, beautiful, comic, heroic, a rare woman whom I seem never to have loved much or honoured enough.

Alfred Edgar Coppard, English author

I press thee to my heart as Duty's faithful child.

Amos Bronson Alcott, American transcendentalist preacher and writer, in his "Sonnet to Louisa May Alcott," his daughter

No one but she could have brought about unity, even harmony, in a family of such strikingly varied personalities. She was the acknowledged head of the household.

Svetlana Alliluyeva, Stalin's
daughter, about her mother

It gives me the greatest pleasure to know that you have discovered the charms of my boy. I never boasted his good qualities to you because I thought you would set it down as a father's fondness, but now that you have found them out yourself, I may say that a more intelligent boy, with a sweeter disposition, does not exist in the world. He is besides noble-minded, honest, and true.

Lord William Russell, British statesman,
to Lady Holland, famous hostess and great
wit of nineteenth-century London

They were all very young and gay and handsome and happy, and they unknowingly provided one of those rare occasions when one can see in one glance that all the hideous sacrifices entailed in their education have not so far been wasted.

Rupert Hart-Davis, British publisher and editor,
about his children after a family reunion

For my sake, pray cherish the person whom I love above all others in the world.

Mme. de Sévigné (Marie de Rabutin-Chantal)
in a letter of 1679 to her daughter

I trust you realize the blessing you have been to us, in the way of high principle and sentiment, and lofty purity of heart, and elegance of taste—to say nothing of a motherly tenderness which has never been surpassed in God's universe, and seldom equalled.

Sophia Hawthorne, wife of Nathaniel, to her mother

I feel perhaps you do not think I appreciate the single-heartedness of your life, your sturdy unselfishness and the sacrifice of ambition for the sake of your family.

Sir Compton Mackenzie to his father

Nothing can come from your workshop, however rough and unfinished, that will not give me more pleasure than the most accurate thing anyone else can write.

Sir Thomas More to his son on receipt of a packet of letters brought to him by a Bristol merchant

He is a creature who speaks in another language from the rest of mankind . . . and would lend life and charm to a treadmill.

Henry James, American novelist, about his brother William, the philosopher

She was an ordinary woman who was extraordinary to me.

Bernard Kops, Canadian writer, about his mother

I think of the music of Mozart when I think of my grandfather.

Elizabeth Goudge

"One generation after another has depended upon its young to equip it with gaiety and enthusiasm, to persuade it that living is a pleasure." And that's one thing that Lynda Bird does for us.

Lady Bird Johnson, writing in
her diary on her daughter
Lynda's twentieth birthday

She brings the sunshine into the house; it is now a pleasure to be there.

Cecil Beaton, English photographer
and designer, about his mother

. . . this . . . little girl, our darling, is become a most intelligent creature, and as gay as a lark, and that in the morning, too, which I do not find so convenient.

Mary Wollstonecraft, the early British
feminist writer, to her American lover
Gilbert Imlay, about their child

She was always a formidable champion of the rights of her own sex. Aunt Bunny was the jolliest, cleverest, and least conventional member of an unconventional family.

Joseph Ackerley, British editor and journalist,
about his mother's youngest sister

I feel refreshed by his young life.
Margaret Fuller Ossoli, American
feminist writer, about her baby

I am pleased to be praised by a man so praised as you, Father.
Cicero, Roman consul, orator, and writer

He is an extraordinarily fine looking man. He is the loveliest man I ever saw or hope to see. . . .
Susy Clemens, Mark Twain's daughter,
in her biography of her father which
she began when she was thirteen years old

I wish I could go on writing to you, it's so consoling. . . .
I can't call for more of your sympathy than you will give, can I? Oh Mother, Mother.
Gertrude Bell, British traveller, archaeologist,
and government official, to her beloved stepmother

You have tangible wealth untold;
Caskets of jewels and coffers of gold.
Richer than I you can never be—
I had a mother who read to me.
Strickland Gillilan in a
poem "The Reading Mother"

You have been the best mother and I believe the best woman in the world.
Dr. Samuel Johnson, British lexicographer,
critic, and conversationalist

My mother, who is between 70 and 80 is *much* younger than I am.
George Bernard Shaw

When I wake in the night I feel my spirits the lighter because you are coming.

William Cowper in a letter to his
cousin and regular correspondent
Lady Hesketh

She was ignorant of life and the world, but possessed a heart full of love.

Hans Christian Andersen, the Danish
author, about his mother.

Dear Mother. Never listens to an argument, never lets logic interfere with the warm impulses of her heart. Singing around the house, a girl's voice still, a bird's heart. Capricious, unpredictable, generous, tactless, stubborn, unreasonable, and lovable mother.

Maurice Wiggin, English journalist

My most humble thanks for the many fine things that you have bestowed on me. And though they be my greatest ornaments . . . they could not give me any contentment, but as I understand they are expressions of your Lordship's favour; a blessing that, above all others in this world, I do with most passion desire.

Lady Dorothy Sidney, later Countess of Sunderland,
to her father the Earl of Leicester

I never saw one so fitted by her grace and playfulness of wit to adorn this life.

Henry James, Sr., about his daughter Alice

I had the best accounts of you. They did not surprise me, for I had unbounded faith in you.

Charles Dickens, the British writer, to his son Alfred Tennyson in 1870

It was from you that I first learned to think, to feel, to imagine, to believe....

John Sterling, nineteenth-century British essayist and poet, in his last letter to his mother who died a week later

I have infinite faith in your innate judgement of yourself and your capabilities. I think you're fortunate in having a sort of in-built gyroscope which . . . does instinctively give you your bearings and your balance.

Kenneth Allsop, English naturalist, filmmaker, and writer, to his twenty-year-old daughter Amanda

I cannot help confessing how sweet and precious and desirable and highly valuable thy love to me is, more than the gold of Ophir....

Lady Rodes, in a letter of 1690, to her son Sir John Rodes

Your friendship will be and is so precious to me, and I desire with all my heart that it should be sincere. It is possible to have the closest intimacy with independence of thought.

Lady Mary Sibylla Holland, the wife of Queen Victoria's chaplain and Canon of Canterbury, in a letter to her sister

She was the last of the generation of real grandmothers. One of the women who made a special grace of age.

Helen Hayes, American actress, about her maternal grandmother

My faith in you is as my affection for you and knows no bounds.

From a letter to Joseph Ackerley from his father

Ill or well, at all ages, you always had and always will have the loveliest and sweetest face possible and appropriate to whatever was or will be its time of life.

Algernon Charles Swinburne, English poet and critic, to his mother

With a mother of different mental caliber I would probably have turned out badly.

Thomas Alva Edison, American inventor, about his mother Nancy Elliott Edison

You are inimitable, irresistible. You are the delight of my life. Such letters, such entertaining letters, as you have lately sent! You are worth your weight in gold, or even in the new silver coinage.

Jane Austen to her niece Fanny

He possessed . . . the gift, so rare that it is always endearing, of being easily and furiously amused, so that it was always a pleasure to be with him and make, or see him, laugh.

Sir Osbert Sitwell, British poet, playwright, and novelist, about his Uncle Raincliffe

The more I see of the world the more I feel thankful for the
bringing up we had, so unworldly, so sound, and so pure.

The thirty-year-old Matthew Arnold,
English author, in a letter from
Wales to his mother on her birthday

I like George much more than most people like their heirs.

Lord Byron about his brother

All three have been, and continue to be, the joy of my life, and
of the many pieces of good fortune that have been poured out on
me I count this as the greatest.

Kenneth Clark, the art historian,
about his children

It makes me very proud of you & makes me feel very happy that my
son should be received with such marvellous enthusiasms of loyalty
and affection . . . members of yr. staff all singing yr. praises. . . .

King George V of England to the Prince of Wales

I must send you another birthday greeting and tell you how much
I love you; that with each day I learn to extol your love and
your worth more and that when I look back over my life, I can
find nothing in your treatment of me that I would alter.

Louis Dembitz Brandeis,
American Supreme Court
Justice, to his mother

Who ran to help me when I fell,
And would some pretty story tell,
Or kiss the place to make it well?
My Mother.

Ann Taylor

Your dear sisters . . . are indeed treasures to me, and their devoted affection outweighs all my misfortunes.

Fanny Trollope, English writer,
to her son Tom, from the United States

My ever-loved mother, I salute you with my affection once more, and thank you for bringing me to this world, and for all your unwearied care over me there.

Thomas Carlyle

My child is a Phenomenon, really the most wonderful Natural Production I ever beheld. . . .

Lady Holland

I was greatly thrilled and touched by the implication which his letter gave that he cared for my opinion as an opinion—the smallest flatteries of one's kin outweigh the acclamations of a multitude.

Alice James about her brother Henry's
letter of twenty-five pages in answer
to a few lines she had written to him

She was the light and not the lamp.
Jessamyn West, American writer,
about her mother

There is nothing I spend so pleaseth me as that which is for you.
If ever I have ability, you will find it; if not, yet shall not
any brother living be better loved than you of me . . . the truly
great part of my comfort is in you.

Sir Philip Sidney to his brother,
Robert, First Earl of Leicester

My mother always seemed to me a fairy princess; a radiant
being possessed of limitless riches and power. . . .

Winston Churchill

You are mine, you are my playfellow, my brother, and we shall
range all over our country together. It is with you that I
see, and that is why I see so clearly . . . in every word I write
and every place I visit I carry you with me.

Katherine Mansfield about her brother
Leslie Beauchamp in her diary in 1916,
immediately after he was killed in the war

He gave me a golden childhood, which is as much as any of us can
ask for. I can remember nothing but happiness and delight in his
company until the world began to be too much for him, when I was
about eleven years old.

Scottie Lanahan about her father F. Scott Fitzgerald

Remember there is no one to whom I shall be prouder to tell of my successes or more willing to confess my failures.

Robert Falcon Scott, Antarctic explorer, in a letter written in October 1911 to his mother from the winter quarters of the British Antarctic Expedition

I should be as happy here as the day is long, if I could hope that I had your smile, your blessing, your sympathy upon it. . . .

Florence Nightingale, British nurse, in a letter to her mother from a nurses' training institute in Dusseldorf

I just want to thank you for everything you've done for me . . . most of all you've given me a good, happy home, with love and THAT is the most important thing. . . . I've been very lucky in having two parents of whom I'm proud not simply as parents, but as people. I hope I can live up to you and make use of all I've got from you.

Amanda Allsop, to her parents after a birthday party they had given for her

Never shall I forget the thousand acts of kindness and affection I have received from you from my earliest to my latest days.

Walter Savage Landor, English poet and prose writer, to his mother

I do not ask for long letters, nor care a farthing about choice phrases. Tell me your domestic news and you will always do me a great happiness.

Sir Walter Scott to his much loved daughter-in-law

"An acquaintance that begins with a compliment," said Oscar Wilde, "is sure to develop into a real friendship." Whether you wholly agree depends on your level of scepticism, but instant attraction is certainly a pleasant way to start a friendship. Many acquaintanceships have grown until the bonds became as strong as those of lovers. The poet Byron, in only nineteen words, charts the history of one such friendship.

Friends are usually able to perceive one another's characteristics with considerable astuteness because they are more detached than either relatives or lovers. Consequently, their pronouncements are likely to be more accurate and trustworthy and their compliments more gratifying to the ego. And if it is a friend's privilege to rebuke when rebuke is called for, it is an even greater privilege—and a joy—freely to express approval and admiration.

Here are compliments from discreet admirers, from adoring fans, from colleagues, and professional peers. The famous pay tribute gracefully and fervently to established celebrities, to people in high places, and also to friends who are not, like themselves, in the public eye. As Abraham Cowley wrote in the seventeenth century, "Nothing so soon the drooping spirit can raise, as praises from the men whom all men praise."

60

For God's sake, madam, when you write to me, talk of yourself; there is nothing I so much desire to hear of; talk a great deal of yourself, that she who I always thought talked best may speak upon the best subject.

Alexander Pope, English satirical poet, to Lady Wortley-Montagu, English poet

I have been into space. I have been to the bottom of the sea, but I have never been as moved as by you tonight.

Scott Carpenter, the American astronaut, to the actress Marlene Dietrich

I was much pleased with him—he is lively, spirited, and quite above all affectation.

Lucy Aiken, nineteenth-century wit and memoirist of royalty, about her meeting with Sir Walter Scott

Among his friends all his geese were swans.

Leonard Woolf, about Alan Rokeby Law, a Cambridge University friend

He is, I believe, the only man living who speaks with equal fluency the American and English languages.

Max Eastman, the American editor and writer, about the popular English writer P.G. Wodehouse

Her constant stream of conversation always impregnated, always had meaning. That lady exerts more *mind* in conversation than any person I have ever met.

> *Dr. Samuel Johnson about Elizabeth Montagu,*
> *a wealthy hostess whose Mayfair salon was*
> *the centre of literary and social life*

You are one of the forces of nature.

> *Jules Michelet, French historian, in a*
> *letter to Alexandre Dumas*

When he was talking to you, you immediately felt that there was no one else in the world he wanted to talk to—you were the centre of his universe.

> *Rex Harrison, the actor, about the*
> *director-producer Alexander Korda*

Your modesty is equal to your valor, and that surpasses the power of any language I possess.

> *John Robinson, Speaker of the Virginia*
> *House of Burgesses, to George Washington*

He is a most wonderful man to have climbed to such a height without ever slipping his foot.

> *Sir Walter Scott*
> *about the Duke of Wellington*

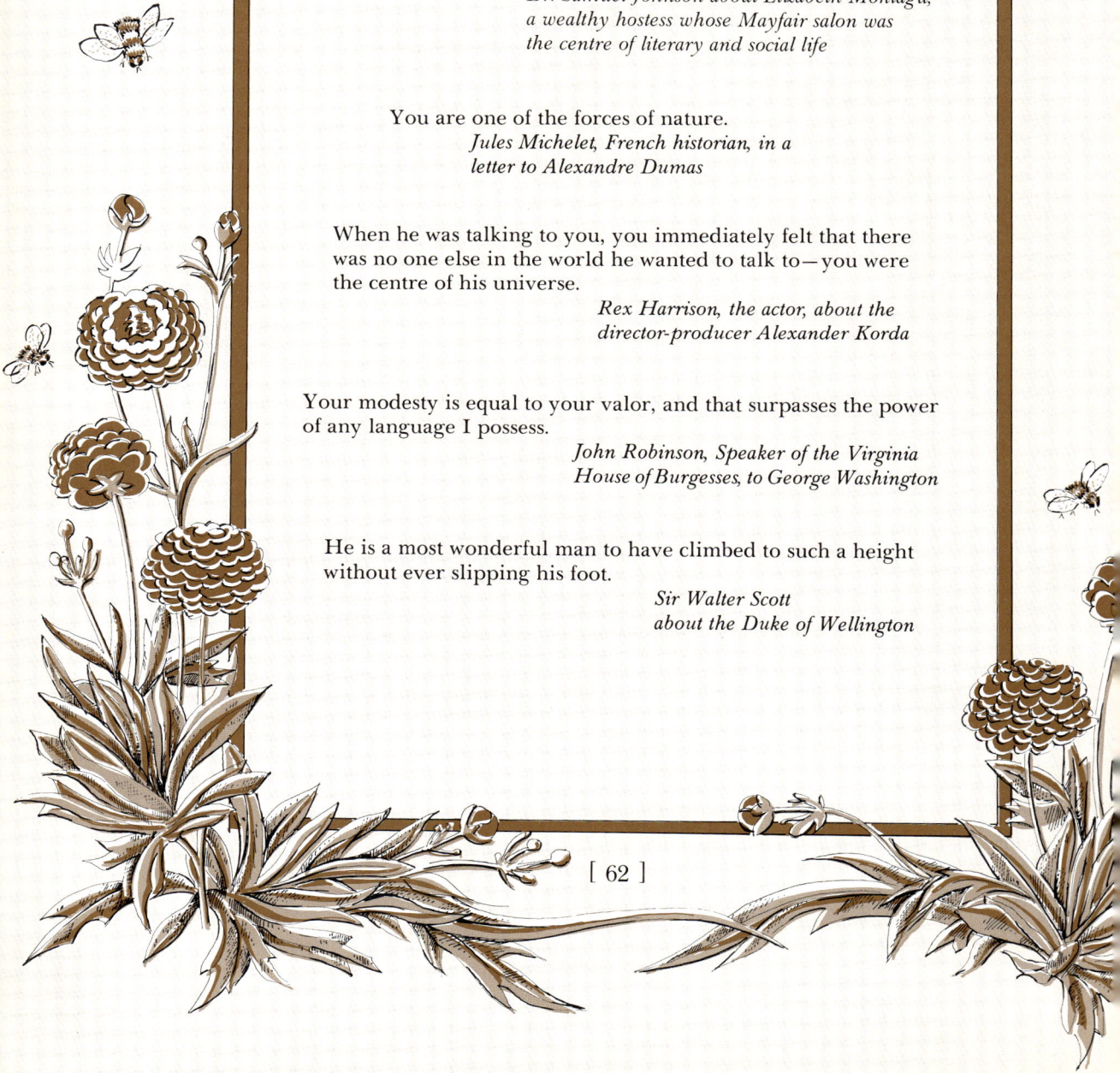

[62]

The last gentleman in Europe.
Ada Leverson, witty English
novelist, about Oscar Wilde

I am at her feet. She has infinite grace of mind, charm,
humour, and deep down kindness. She puts everyone at ease
immediately, without apparent effort.
Noel Coward about the
Queen Mother after a
lunch party in Jamaica in 1963

He is the first Harvard man to know enough to drop three
syllables when he has something to say.
American humorist Will Rogers about
President Franklin Delano Roosevelt

Churchill is a prize, heartrending example of the kind of
person I would most like to be.
Richard Burton, Welsh actor,
about Sir Winston Churchill

. . . (he) has the quickest mind of anyone I have ever known;
like the greatest of chess players he sees in a flash six
moves ahead of the ordinary player and one move ahead of
all the other Grand Masters.

Leonard Woolf about the
philosopher Bertrand Russell

Her voice in conversation . . . has a melting quality that penetrates the senses, as some soothing ointment goes through the skin. Her eyes do the rest—complete the charm begun by voice, expression, and a thoroughly natural and sympathetic manner. . . . She is a delightful, womanly woman.

Kate Chopin, American novelist, critic, and short story writer, about fellow-novelist Ruth McEnery Stuart

If you were to make the little fishes talk, they would talk like whales.

Oliver Goldsmith, Irish poet, dramatist, and novelist, to Dr. Samuel Johnson

She was of another texture to those around her, radiant, translucent, intense.

Anonymous description of Lady Randolph Churchill

How can you divine my tastes so exactly—what's more, add to them your own exquisitry?

Virginia Woolf to her friend Ethel Sands, acknowledging a gift

She is the perfect example of how to grow old, and proves how wrong it is to make too much effort in the ways of artifice.

Viscountess Head about the English actress Cathleen Nesbitt

I love her vivid awareness of the trembling beauty of life.
Lady Ottoline Morrell, Bloomsbury
hostess, about Katherine Mansfield

When I came here my first thoughts were of you, my dear and excellent friend; the joy of finding you again was the warmest feeling I know. . . .

Archduchess Sophie of Wurtemberg
to Lady William Russell

That woman is a blessing to me, and I never see her without being the better for her company.

William Cowper about
his friend Mrs. William Unwin

I shall just go on rejoicing in the fact of you.
Katherine Mansfield to her friend
Anne Estelle Rice, the American painter

The affection and respect I bear you are too great for easy composition . . . it should be a consolation to you that while you go everywhere and know and are known by more kinds of men than any, perhaps, of your contemporaries, you are everywhere admired, everywhere respected, and, by those who have the honour of your acquaintance, loved. . . . That your talents are found well used, your breeding maintained, your honour beyond question, your company desired, and your absence always regretted. Look round you and ask of how many men such things can be said.

Hilaire Belloc, English author, to
Sir Evan Charteris, lawyer and art connoisseur

He is the biggest man you have on your side of the water by a damn sight, and don't you forget it.

Rudyard Kipling about
Mark Twain, in a letter written
to his American publisher

I have need of your warming and revivifying rays; and I hope I shall have them frequently.

Samuel Johnson to his companion
and biographer James Boswell

The nobility of his manner is a product of the nobility of his heart.

Gustav Flaubert about his
good friend Maxime du Camp

You are the only subject I shake hands with.

William IV, Great Britain's "Sailor
King," to the Duke of Wellington,
the hero of the Battle of Waterloo

His worst is better than any other person's best.

William Hazlitt, English critic and
essayist, about Sir Walter Scott

If Beethoven is a miracle of humanity, Bach is a miracle of God.

Gioacchino Rossini, the
Italian operatic composer

I have never known anyone more capable of endearing himself to others. And this was not only the result of his great warmth, charm, and touching funniness. I have not known anyone with a more bold and childlike innocence of mind. The exuberance of his strong physique, of his strong physical life, never marred or blurred that.

Edith Sitwell about Dylan Thomas
the Welsh poet, whose great talent
she was one of the first to recognize

A man must be a real hero to resist such a letter as yours.
Thomas Hardy, nineteenth-century English
author, to an unidentified correspondent

. . . a solid-boned, athletic-looking youngster of eighty-two. . . .
Lewis Mumford about Lord Bryce,
British journalist, historian, and diplomat

His *voice* first attracted my attention, his *countenance* fixed it, and his *manners* attached me to him for ever.
Lord Byron about
a Trinity College classmate

He is one of those noble-hearted young men to whom the happiness and freedom of mankind is a goal they never lose sight of. His manners are those of a gentleman and a man of the world, but they are tempered by a delicate moral sense which pervades his whole personality and radiates charmingly from his speech and behaviour.
Johann Wolfgang von Goethe,
about Cavaliere Filangieri,
a young Italian writer

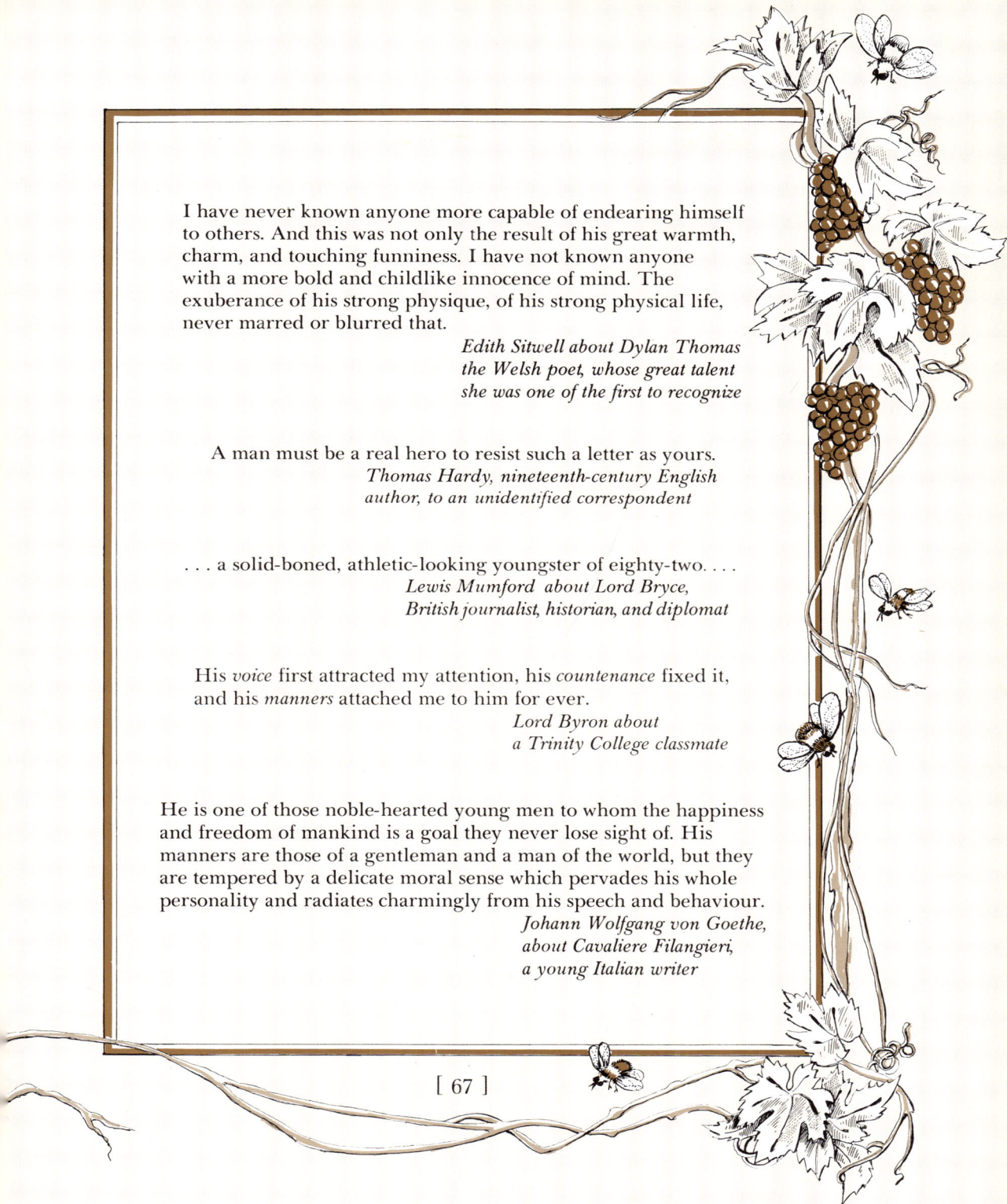

Her beauty and her intelligence both seem to be indestructible. . . .

Noel Coward about Lady Diana Cooper, wife of
Alfred Duff Cooper, diplomat and political figure

Like every real aristocrat she had the ability to put everyone
at his ease and to meet any situation.

Richard Aldington, English poet
and novelist, about Natalie Barney

It is impossible to believe that you will be eighty tomorrow,
but I like to think of it, for it gives most people an opportunity
of seeing how life should be lived without being spent.

Margot Asquith, wife of the prime minister,
to William Gladstone, British statesman and
long-time prime minister

To be seventy years young is sometimes far more cheerful and
hopeful than to be forty years old.

Oliver Wendell Holmes, American man of letters,
to Julia Ward Howe, writer, lecturer, women's
suffrage leader, and author of the poem "Battle
Hymn of the Republic," on her seventieth birthday

If I wrote this in verse, I would tell you, you are like the sun;
and while men imagine you to be retired or absent, you are hourly
exerting your indulgence and bringing things to maturity for
their advantage. Of all the world, you are the man (without
flattery) who serve your friends with the least ostentation; it
is almost ingratitude to thank you, considering your temper.

Alexander Pope to Jonathan Swift

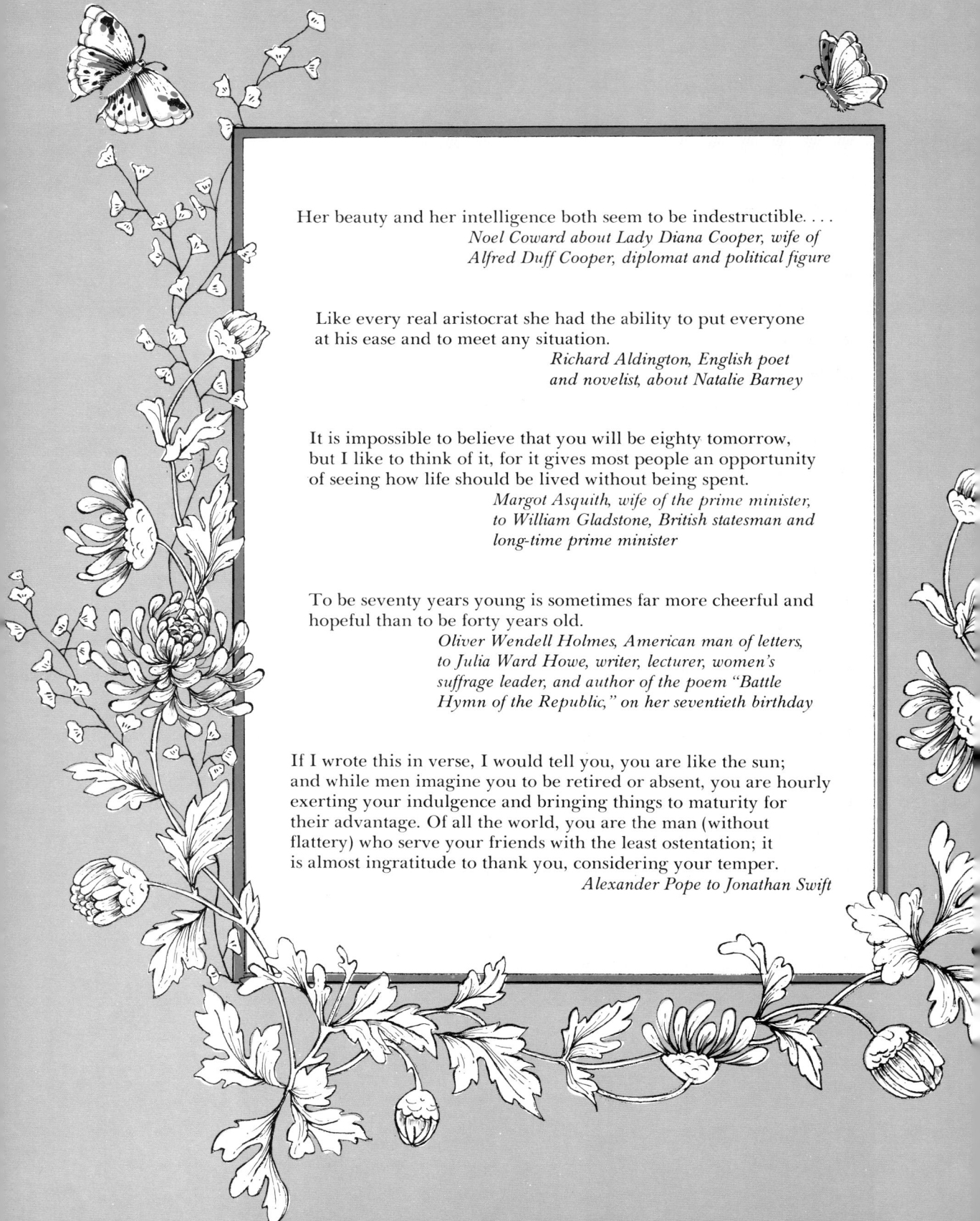

Such agreeable company and conversation will turn Lent into a festival; but let it do so, I will run the risk of the punishment, if you, Sir, will make the pilgrimage.

Lady Luxborough to William Shenstone,
the eighteenth-century English poet

The sight of him is peace.

Mark Twain about Harry H. Rogers, a wealthy admirer who had given time, money, and labour to save him from bankruptcy, yet was known on Wall Street as a ruthless pirate

We could not be farther apart as human beings and yet I find myself completely at ease with him and stimulated by his enthusiasm. For he has this golden quality of being able to enjoy life.

Cecil Beaton about painter David Hockney

Her liveliness is of that kind which shows at once it is connected with thorough principle, and is not liable to be influenced by fashionable caprice.

Sir Walter Scott about
the Duchess of Northumberland

He left scarcely any style of writing untouched, and touched nothing that he did not adorn.

Dr. Samuel Johnson's epitaph
on Oliver Goldsmith

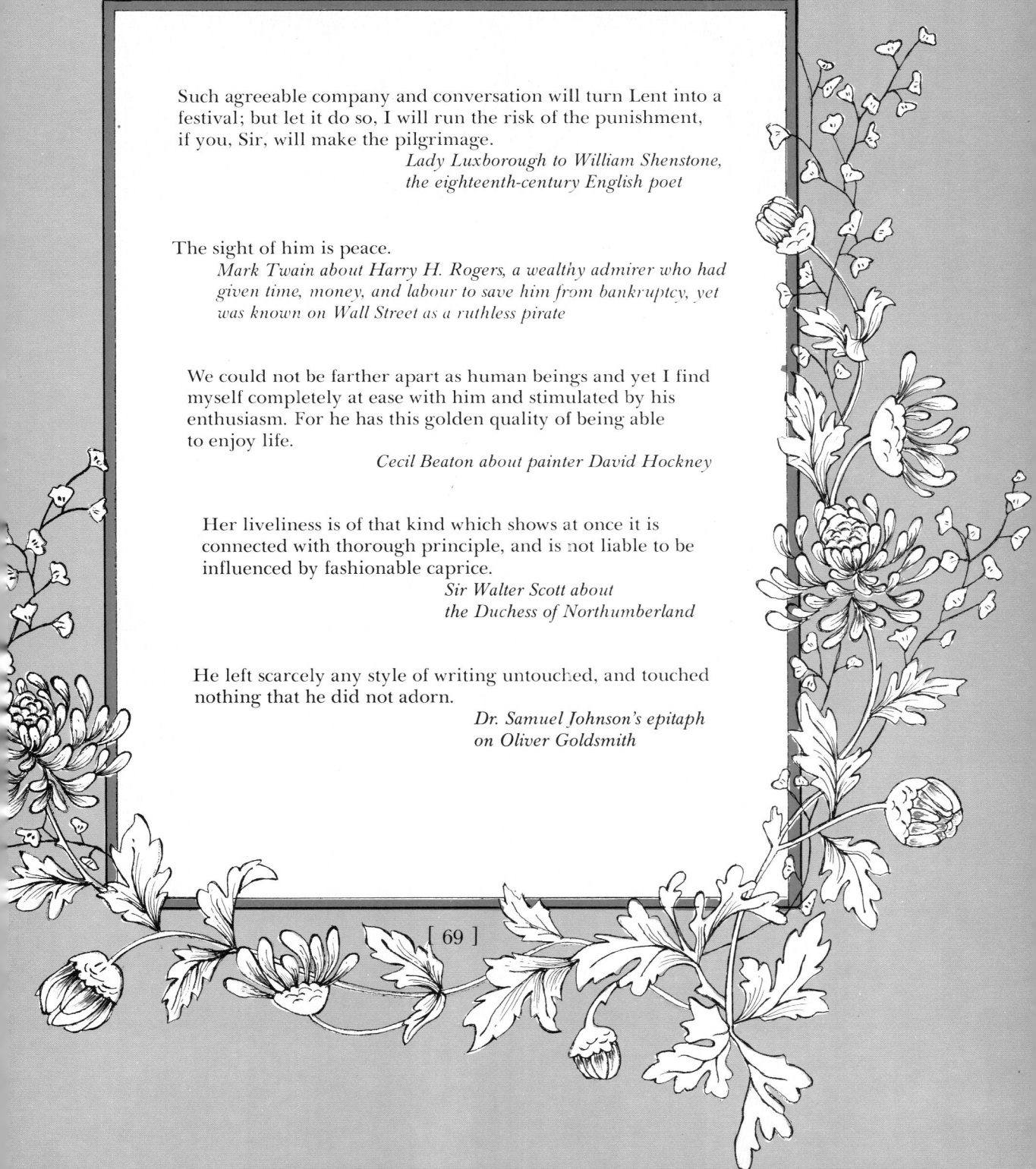

[69]

His only fault is that he has no fault.
Pliny the Younger, Roman writer

You are, I believe, one of the kindest of women, one
of the best balanced, with that maternal quality that
of all others I need and adore. . . .
Virginia Woolf to Dame Ethel Smyth, a composer

These may be, without question,
Rather bad for your digestion.
But the powers have not sent me
To preach sermons; they've but lent me
A keen desire to please you
Now and always without end,
And a little wish to tease you
With the fondness of a friend.
*Kate Chopin sent this poem
to her friend "Billy," with
a box of cigars*

I . . . would as freely give you my heart in a dish as he (Herod)
did another's head. . . . You may easily imagine how desirous I must
be of corresponding with a person who had taught me long ago that
it was as possible to esteem at first sight, as to love, and who
has since ruined me for all the conversation of one sex, and
almost all the friendship of the other. . . . Books have lost their
effect upon me, and I was convinced, since I saw you, that there
is something more powerful than philosophy, and, since I heard
you, that here is one alive wiser than all the sages.
Alexander Pope to Lady Wortley-Montagu

You have literally bewitched me with some of the melodies in your new pieces. I have not been able to get them out of my head for days.

Clara Schumann to
Johannes Brahms, German composer

I can scarcely admit a doubt that the lady will know how to value those qualities in you which I place far above those that have justly gained you worldly distinction, and for whose deficiency no intellectual eminence could compensate.

Isabella Lawrence to Sir William Rowan Hamilton, in a
letter congratulating him on his forthcoming marriage

By God you are a splendid fellow, a man worth many oxen!

Hilaire Belloc to Gilbert Moorhead

His visions are authentic, profound and beautiful. Even among visionaries he is rare, for he is a visionary not with an unearthly or heavenly vision, but a human vision. He is a seer with astonishing compassion for human beings.

James Dickey, American poet, about another American
poet James Wright, a Pulitzer Prize winner

The height on which he stands has not made him giddy.

Lord Byron about Francis,
Lord Jeffrey, founder and
editor of "Edinburgh Review"

Come home, for 'tis dull living without you.
Hester Thrale Piozzi in a letter
to her friend Dr. Samuel Johnson

What pleasure I have had in seeing and talking with you, I will not attempt to say. I shall never forget it as long as I live.
Charles Dickens, to the American author Washington Irving

His conversation is very various and natural, full of information, given for the sake of those to whom he speaks, never for display.
Maria Edgeworth, English novelist,
about Lord Lansdowne

I think myself extremely obliged by you in all points, especially for your kind and honourable information and advice in a matter of the utmost concern to me, which I shall ever acknowledge as the highest proof at once of your friendship, justice and sincerity....
You have yourself obliged me more than any man, which is, that you have shewed me many of my faults, of which as you are the more an implacable enemy, by so much the more are you a kind friend to me.
Alexander Pope to William Wycherly, the dramatist

She looks like the pungent perfume of some exotic essence....
Jean Cocteau, French poet and artist,
about the ballet dancer Ida Rubinstein

My friendship with you was—is—the great blessing of my life. I think I need not say whether every word of yours is precious to me.
Julia Wedgwood, the English writer,
to Robert Browning in 1869

Jenny kissed me when we met,
Jumping from the chair she sat in;
Time, you thief, who love to get
Sweets into your list, put that in:
Say I'm weary, say I'm sad,
Say that health and wealth have missed me,
Say I'm growing old, but add,
Jenny kissed me.

Rondeau for Jane Carlyle,
by her friend Leigh Hunt,
poet, essayist, and editor

When I first met him it was like a personal reward and the renewal of intimacy has been one of the prizes of life.

William Rothenstein, the English painter,
about the poet Rabindranath Tagore

He is so fearfully nice *and* kind *and* has read Tolstoi — what a pearl to find in these oceans of sillies!

Katherine Mansfield about her doctor

His low spirits were much more uproarious and enlivening than anybody else's high spirits.

G.K. Chesterton, English journalist
and writer, about Hilaire Belloc

This woman teaches people to think who would not do it of themselves, or who have forgotten how.

Napoleon Bonaparte about Mme. de Staël

He is not deep but remarkable. A hasty kind of genius.

T.E. Lawrence about
Noel Coward after his first
encounter with him in 1930

Dr. Johnson used to say that he never in his life had eaten as much fruit as he desired. I think I never talked to you as much as I desired.

Dr. Benjamin Jowett, Greek scholar
and Master of Balliol College, Oxford,
to Margot Asquith

I still see him as a prancing faun, thinly disguised by conventional apparel.

Harold Acton, British author, about
the novelist Evelyn Waugh, who had
been his boon companion at Oxford

His head is charming, lit by a perfect smile, by a smile to illustrate the word "smile" in a dictionary.

Adrienne Monnier, owner of the famous
Paris bookshop, describing Maurice Chevalier

He is a wonderfully sympathetic friend and his rectitude of mind is enchanting.

Lady Ottoline Morrell about
Bertrand Russell who had been her lover

I embrace you as a sister of my spirit.
Paul Valery, French man of letters, in
a letter of 1940 to the Argentinian
editor and intellectual Victoria Ocampo

Is not my soul laid open before you in these veracious pages?
This is the pleasure of corresponding with a friend, where doubt
and distrust have no place, and everything is said as it is thought.
These are the letters by which souls are united, and by which
minds naturally in unison move each as they are moved themselves.
Dr. Samuel Johnson to Hester Thrale

. . . a being who is, physically, of the lily tribe, but with
a human heart and mind.
Edith Sitwell, English poet, about Greta Garbo

I am glad your travels delighted you; improve you I am
sure they could not.
Alexander Pope to Dr. John Arbuthnot,
a Scottish physician

. . . the first highly cultivated and brilliant woman I had ever
known. I stood a little in awe of her, as I always did in the
presence of intellectual superiority, and liked best to sit
silent and listen to a conversation which I still think almost
the best of its day.

Edith Wharton, the American novelist,
about Violet Paget who wrote under the
pseudonym of Vernon Lee

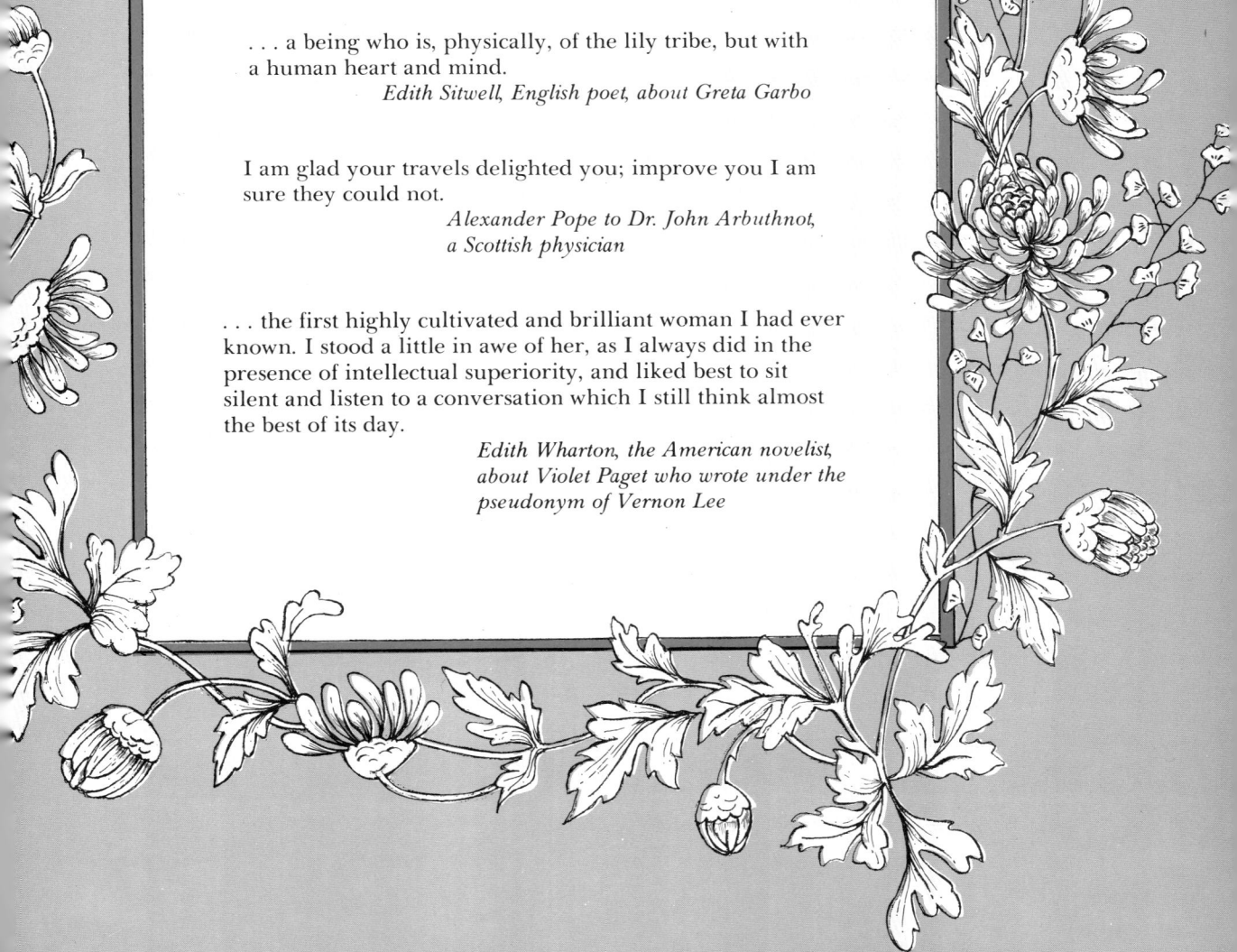

Compliments?

A rose does have thorns and a compliment has many uses
—not the least of which is to disguise an insult. Sometimes
a compliment begins innocently and then within the blink
of an eye or the drop of a comma, it takes on a tinge of
mischief, an edge of malice, a drop of acid. Like Gertrude
Lawrence's cable to Noel Coward on an opening night, a
devilish little barb or sting in the tail can, with astonishing
swiftness, flip a compliment neatly inside out.

Probably only saints—or dullards—are able to resist
throwing a verbal dart when it is well deserved, especially if
it springs to the lips in epigrammatic form. Many a wit has
depended for fame on a sharp eye and a sharper tongue—
Oscar Wilde, Winston Churchill, and Dorothy Parker not
least among them.

The world is definitely a more entertaining place for the
presence of such quick thinkers. Whether their sallies are
read or overheard, they offer us harmless outlets for our
own impulses to malice.

[76]

He is every other inch a gentleman.
Rebecca West, the British writer

She ran the whole gamut of emotions from A to B.
Dorothy Parker, American writer and wit,
about the actress Katherine Hepburn

You have too luscious a bosom to keep the conversation general.
Mme. Aubernon's advice to a young
matron ambitious to run a salon

He hasn't an enemy in the world, and none of his friends like him.
Oscar Wilde about his
countryman George Bernard Shaw

I'm very proud of you. You managed to play the first act of my little comedy tonight with all the Chinese flair and light-hearted brilliance of Lady Macbeth.
Noel Coward to the leading lady after a
disastrous opening night of "Blithe Spirit"

Like the British Constitution, she owes her success in practice to her inconsistencies in principle.
Thomas Hardy

She has never been any closer to life than the dinner table.
Janet Flanner about Elsa Maxwell,
famous for her party-giving

He has occasional flashes of silence that make his conversation perfectly delightful.

> *Sydney Smith, English clergyman, essayist,*
> *and wit, about the British writer Thomas Macaulay*

He will even tell a lie when it is not convenient to. That is the sign of a great artist, you know!

> *Gore Vidal, the American writer,*
> *about Richard Nixon*

Your play is delightful, and there's nothing that can't be fixed.

> *Gertrude Lawrence, the British*
> *actress, in a cable to Noel Coward*

He never said a foolish thing, nor ever did a wise one.

> *Epitaph on King Charles II*

He is a sceptic, cynic, sophist, as well as artist, who moves at ease among philosophical generalizations, and is the dupe of nothing—except a well-turned phrase.

> *A.B. Walkley, the English dramatist*
> *and critic, about Oscar Wilde*

A great unrecognized incapacity.

> *Prince Otto von Bismarck, first chancellor of the German*
> *Empire, referring to Napoleon III in a letter of 1862,*
> *while he was minister to France*

He has the most remarkable and deductive genius—and I should say about the smallest in the world.

> *Lytton Strachey about the English critic.*
> *essayist, and caricaturist, Max Beerbohm*

He's always backing into the limelight.

> *Said about T.E. Lawrence, Lawrence of Arabia*

It must have taken him a great deal of pains to become what we now see him. Such an excess of stupidity is not in nature.

> *Samuel Johnson about his*
> *contemporary the actor Thomas Sheridan*

In defeat unbeatable, in victory unbearable.

> *Winston Churchill about Montgomery of Alamein*

My wife is one of the best women on this continent, although she isn't always as gentle as a lamb with mint sauce.

> *Charles Farrar Browne, the nineteenth-*
> *century American humorist who wrote*
> *under the pseudonym Artemus Ward*

Sharp as a needle are her words;
Her wit, like pepper, bites. . . .

> *John Gay, the eighteenth-century*
> *English poet and playwright*

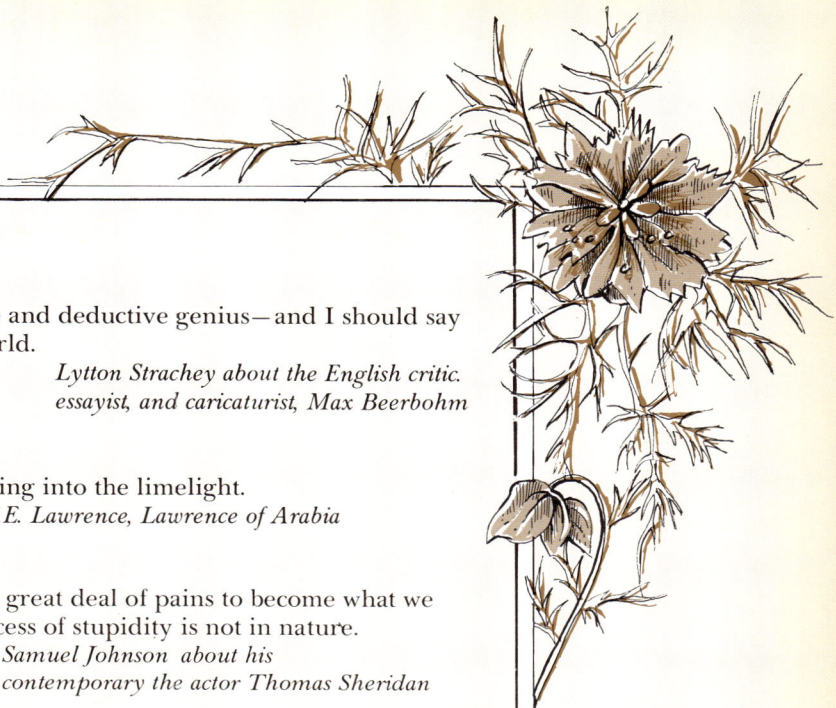

I thought he was a young man of promise; but it appears he was a young man of promises.

> *A.J. Balfour, English philosopher and statesman, about the young Winston Churchill*

For her, each new affair was an encampment set up along the way; sometimes a palace, sometimes a tent, but always a supreme refuge.

> *Lesley Blanch about Jane Digby, the Victorian adventuress in the Arab world*

The time was out of joint, and he was only too delighted to have been born to set it right.

> *Lytton Strachey, the twentieth-century English writer, about Richard Hurrell Froude, the Victorian clergyman*

He had no talent, but he wrote a book in which his earnestness and his sincerity, his thoughtfulness and his integrity, were so evident that, although it was quite unreadable, no one could fail to be impressed by it.

> *Somerset Maugham, the British writer, about Charles Lamb, the popular English essayist*

It was not a bosom to repose upon, but it was a capital bosom to hang jewels on.

> *Charles Dickens*

I felt that an angel food cake baked by her
would never dare collapse.
> *Said by O. Henry, the American
> short story writer, about Eleanor
> Nagle, the beauty editor of the
> "Chicago News Flash"*

One of those characteristic British faces that, once seen,
are never remembered.

> *Oscar Wilde*

This Adonis in loveliness was a corpulent man of fifty.
> *English writer Leigh Hunt said this about
> the Prince Regent, later George IV; and
> as a result, was sent to prison*

I don't object to the Old Man's always having the
ace of trumps up his sleeve, but merely to his belief
that God Almighty put it there.
> *Henry Labouchere, the
> British statesman, about
> William Gladstone*

She seemed timeless. . . . As she scratched her head and fixed you
with her eagle eye, you felt you were taking tea with a monument.
> *Harold Acton about Gertrude Stein,
> the American writer and art patron*

She's more of a man than I expected.
Remarked by Henry James after
reading Queen Victoria's letters

He is a man of the world, with all the narrowness that belongs
to those imprisoned on that planet.
G.K. Chesterton about his
contemporary, the writer Rudyard Kipling

A legend in his own lunchtime.
Christopher Wordsworth, literary critic,
about Clifford Makins, sporting journalist

. . . the first man to have cut a swathe through the theatre and
left it strewn with virgins.
Frank Harris about George Bernard Shaw

A modest little man with much to be modest about.
Winston Churchill about Clement Atlee,
labour leader and politician

He never spares himself in conversation. He gives himself so
generously that hardly anybody else is permitted to give
anything in his presence.
Aneurin Bevan, the British statesman,
about Winston Churchill

I like you so much that sometimes it's an effort to
remember that you're a woman at all.
British playwright Terence Rattigan

What a terrible look he has! That man can speak only to God.
French novelist François Mauriac
about the writer Paul Claudel

He is a worthy Man; I do not believe he has a Fault,
except that of desiring to be what he is not.
Juliet, Lady Catesby, an eighteenth-century
society belle, about an acquaintance

. . . the only man in America who could sit on a fence
and see himself go by.
Ed Howe, the American journalist,
about the historian Henry Adams

He is a self-made man and worships his creator.
John Bright, orator and statesman, about
Benjamin Disraeli

When he waved to you or with a broad gesture took off his hat, you
felt that it was incredibly affable of him to take any notice
of human beings.

Somerset Maugham about the Vicomte
de Steenvoorde, who represented
important French interests in China

She is a Jewish princess by marriage.
Overheard at a cocktail party

Mr. Chamberlain loves the working man; he loves to see him work.
*Winston Churchill about fellow-statesman Joseph
Chamberlain who was instrumental in passing
the 1897 Workmen's Compensation Act*

He always hits the nail on the head, but it doesn't go in
any further.
*Anonymous comment about Stanley Baldwin,
the British statesman and writer*

She's the sort of woman who lives for others—you can
tell the others by their hunted expression.
C.S. Lewis, the English writer

Wagner has lovely moments, but awful quarters of an hour.
*Gioacchino Rossini about the German
composer Richard Wagner*

For the last twenty years her age has been legendary.
*Janet Flanner about Elsie de Wolfe,
Lady Mendl, international celebrity
as actress, decorator, and hostess*

What time he can spare from the adornment of his person
he devotes to the neglect of his duties.
William Hepworth Thompson

This Englishwoman is so refined
She has no bosom and no behind.
Stevie Smith, the English poet

He's a man of great common sense and good taste—meaning thereby
a man without originality or moral courage.
George Bernard Shaw

The only woman I know with a male sense of humour.
Constant Lambert, English composer and conductor

. . . a remarkably handsome man when he is in full tide of
sermonizing, and his face is lit up with animation, but he
is as homely as a singed cat when he isn't doing anything.
*Mark Twain about Henry Ward Beecher, a leader
in the movement for the abolition of slavery*

His remarks wore monocles.
Harold Acton about Somerset Maugham

He is invited to all the great houses in England—once.
*Oscar Wilde about his contemporary,
the Irish author Frank Harris*

The Emperor becomes his robes as if he had been hatched in them.

Lord Byron about Napoleon Bonaparte

. . . the most enchanting, wonderful, delicious human being in the world . . . until I slipped a wedding ring on her finger.

*Leland Hayward, literary agent
and producer, about his wife,
the actress Margaret Sullavan*

They say I never forget a face, but I'll make an exception of yours.

Groucho Marx

A man to whom heaven had given the powers of a supreme genius, and hell the soul of a commercial traveller.

Oscar Wilde about Frederick the Great

First in ability on the list of second-rate men.

*Anonymous comment about Chester Alan Arthur,
twenty-first president of the United States*

He is a most remarkable man—and I am the other one. Between us, we cover all knowledge: he knows all that can be known and I know the rest.

Mark Twain about Rudyard Kipling

She wears her clothes as if they were thrown on her with a pitchfork.

Jonathan Swift

At the age of eighteen or nineteen his literary taste was completely formed. He was discriminating to a degree that killed appreciation. Everything froze at his touch.

Harold Acton about Peter Quennell,
an influential English literary figure

I wish this dear, good Harriet would go and be happy somewhere else.

Thomas Carlyle about Harriet Martineau,
English novelist and economist

Nothing will convince me that he is not a fundamentally simple man. Under all his affectation and vanity there is a core of real simplicity.

Harold Nicolson, British statesman,
about prime minister Ramsay MacDonald

I could have wept, parting with him, but I could not get at my handkerchief without unbuttoning my boatcloak and that was inconvenient.

Jane Welsh Carlyle about an
acquaintance met on a journey

. . . a confectioner's goddess of vanilla-flavoured ice cream.

Edith Sitwell describing Mary Pickford

The effect upon women is such that they want to go right out and get him and bring him home stuffed.

Dorothy Parker about her fellow-
American, writer Ernest Hemingway

At any gathering he is about as anonymous and inconspicuous as a buffalo bull in a herd of range cattle.

Stanley Walker, American writer, about
Wendell Wilkie, Republican presidential
nominee in 1940

She pleases all Eyes, but she pleases the Eyes only.

Juliet, Lady Catesby
about a "friend"

He has a brilliant mind until he makes it up.

Margot Asquith
about E.F. Smith, Earl of Birkenhead

He will develop into a remarkable man, and I shall be the first to applaud and admire him—from afar!

Ivan Turgenev, Russian novelist,
about Leo Tolstoi with whom he had
a lifelong love-hate relationship

To my daughter, Leonora, without whose never-failing sympathy and encouragement this book would have been finished in half the time.

A dedication by P.G. Wodehouse

Of course he was a wonderful all-round man, but the act of walking round him always tired me.

Max Beerbohm about the
British artist William Morris

Her marriages were adventures and her friendships enduring.
George Bernard Shaw about Ellen Terry

He was the life and death of every party because he couldn't stop talking.
Alan Searle, Somerset Maugham's secretary and companion, about Jean Cocteau

I had a kind of feeling that he could always score me off with such grace, good humour, and wit that I would never discover it.
Margot Asquith about Lord Salisbury

She is a little formidable, both in her affection and her hatred. I am suffering at the moment from her affection.
Aldous Huxley, English writer, about one of his aunts

Come again when you have a little less time.
Walter Sickert, the British painter, to the young English writer Denton Welch

He has a transcendental gift, even when he is writing sense, of making it appear to be nonsense.
Edith Sitwell about F.R. Leavis, the literary critic

He has delusions of adequacy.
Walter Kerr, New York drama critic, about an actor

INDEX OF COMPLIMENTS

William Cobbett (1763-1835)
about his wife, 23
Jean Cocteau (1889-1963)
about Ida Rubenstein, 72
William Congreve (1670-1729)
to Arabella Hunt, 20
Alfred Edgar Coppard (1878-1957)
about his mother, 48
Noel Coward (1899-1973)
to an actress, 77
about Lady Diana Cooper, 68
his mother, 44
the Queen Mother, 63
Abraham Cowley (1618-1667)
about a woman, 23
William Cowper (1731-1800)
to his cousin Lady Hesketh, 53
about a kinsman, 44
Mrs. William Unwin, 65
George Crabbe (1754-1832)
about his wife Sarah Elmy,
29
Cyrano de Bergerac (1619-1655)
to Roxane, 15
Charles Dickens (1812-1870)
to his son Alfred Tennyson
Dickens, 54
Washington Irving, 72
about a woman, 80
James Dickey (1923-   )
about James Wright, 71
Benjamin Disraeli (1804-1881)
about his wife Mary Ann, 20
to his wife, 12
his sister Sarah, 47
Mary Ann Disraeli (1782-1872)
about her husband Benjamin,
39
John Donne (1573-1631)
to Lady Magdalen Herbert, 14
Sir Arthur Conan Doyle
(1859-1930)
to his wife, 13
Juliette Drouet (1806-1883)
to her lover Victor Hugo, 34
Alexandre Dumas (1802-1870)
to his son Alexandre, 44
Thomas D'Urfey (1653-1723)
to "Chloë," 20
Max Eastman (1883-1969)
about P.G. Wodehouse, 61
Maria Edgeworth (1767-1849)
about Lord Lansdowne, 72
Thomas Alva Edison (1849-1931)
about his mother Nancy, 55
King Edward VIII (1894-1972)
about his fiancée Wallis Simpson,
13
George Eliot (Mary Ann Evans)
(1819-1880)
to George Henry Lewes, 34

Janet Flanner (1892-   )
about Elsa Maxwell, 77
Elsie de Wolfe, Lady Mendl, 84
Gustave Flaubert (1821-1880)
about Maxime du Camp, 66
to his mistress Louise Colet, 14
Margaret Fuller, Marchioness
Ossoli (1810-1877)
about her son, 51
Jill Furse (1915-1945)
to her husband Laurence Whistler,
40
Léon Gambetta (1838-1882)
to his mistress Léonie Léon, 23
John Gay (!685-1732)
to a woman, 79
King George V (1865-1936)
to his son the Prince of Wales,
56
King George VI (1895-1952)
to his daughter Princess
Elizabeth, 43
Strickland Gillilan (1860-1954)
about his mother, 52
Johann Wolfgang von Goethe
(1749-1832)
about Cavaliere Filangieri, 67
Vincent van Gogh (1853-1890)
to his brother Theo, 46
Oliver Goldsmith (1728-1774)
to Samuel Johnson, 64
Elizabeth Goudge (1900-   )
about her grandfather, 50
her mother, 43
Hafiz (14th century)
to a woman, 22
Emma, Lady Hamilton (1761-1815)
to her husband Sir William
Hamilton, 31
her lover Horatio, Lord
Nelson, 40
Thomas Hardy (1840-1928)
to a correspondent, 67
about a woman, 77
Frank Harris (1854-1931)
about George Bernard Shaw, 82
Rex Harrison (1908-   )
about Alexander Korda, 62
Rupert Hart-Davis (1907-   )
about his children, 49
Warren Hastings (1732-1818)
to his wife, 29
Nathaniel Hawthorne (1804-1864)
to his fiancée Sophia Amelia
Peabody, 11
Sophie Hawthorne (1811-1871)
to her mother, 50
Helen Hayes (1900-   )
about her husband Charles
MacArthur, 37
her grandmother, 55

Leland Hayward (1902-1971)
about his wife Margaret Sullavan,
86
William Hazlitt (1778-1830)
about Sir Walter Scott, 66
Viscountess Head (20th century)
about Cathleen Nesbitt, 64
Lillian Hellman (1906-   )
about Dashiell Hammett, 41
Heloise (1097-1164)
to her husband Abelard, 37
O. Henry (William Sidney Porter)
(1862-1910)
about Eleanor Nagle, 81
Robert Herrick (1591-1674)
to "Anthea," 26
John Hervey (1696-1743)
to his wife Elizabeth, 28
James Hogg (1770-1835)
to his fiancée Margaret Philips,
17
Lady Mary Sibylla Holland
(19th century)
to her sister, 54
Lady Holland (1780-1845)
about her child, 57
Oliver Wendell Holmes (1809-1894)
to Julia Ward Howe, 68
Homer (3rd century B.C.)
about Helen of Troy, 12
Edgar Watson Howe (1853-1937)
about Henry Adams, 83
Victor Hugo (1802-1885)
to his fiancée Adele Foucher, 15
David Hume (1711-1776)
to Mme. de Boufflers, 24
Leigh Hunt (1784-1859)
to Jane Carlyle, 73
about the Prince Regent, 81
Aldous Huxley (1894-1963)
about his aunt, 89
Thomas Henry Huxley (1825-1895)
about his fiancée Henrietta
Ann Heathorn, 17
Robert J. Ingersoll (1833-1899)
to his daughter Eva Ingersoll, 46
Alice James (1848-1892)
about her brother Henry, 57
Henry James, Sr. (1811-1882)
about his daughter Alice, 53
Henry James, Jr. (1843-1916)
about his brother William, 50
Queen Victoria, 82
Mary James (1811-1881)
about her husband Henry
James, Sr., 33
Thomas Jefferson (1743-1826)
to his daughter, 46
Jennie Jerome (1854-1921)
to her fiancé Lord Randolph
Churchill, 40

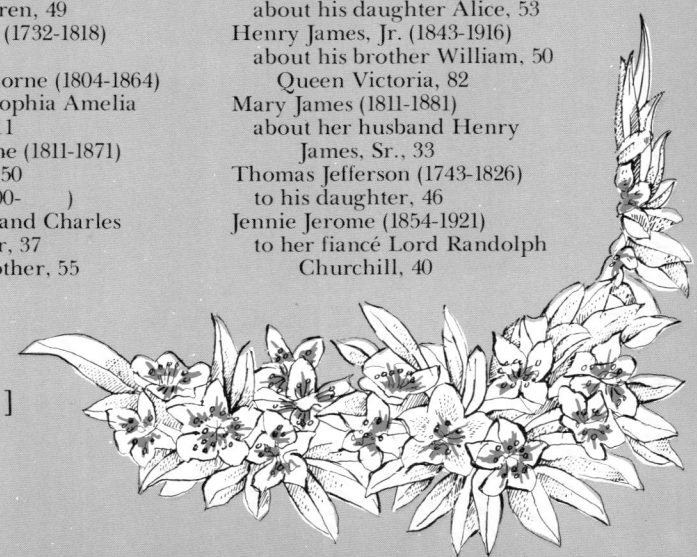

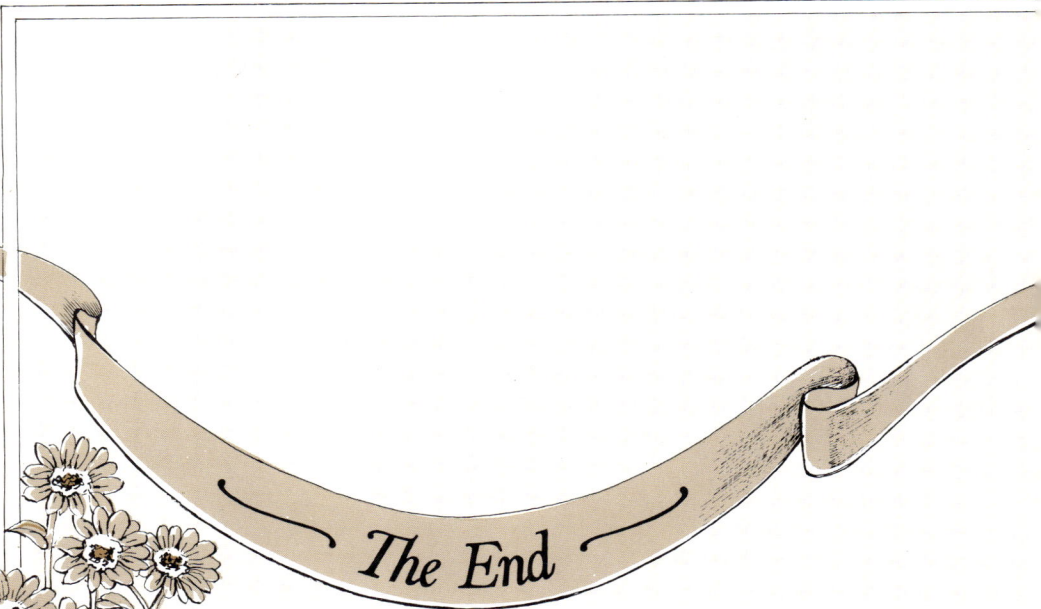

The End